UNDERSTANDING
THE PROFESSIONAL BUYER

What every sales professional should know
about how the modern buyer thinks and behaves

Peter Cheverton
Jan Paul van der Velde

KoganPage

LONDON PHILADELPHIA NEW DELHI

First published in Great Britain and the United States in 2011 by Kogan Page Limited

120 Pentonville Road	525 South 4th Street, #241	4737/23 Ansari Road
London N1 9JN	Philadelphia PA 19147	Daryaganj
United Kingdom	USA	New Delhi 110002
www.koganpage.com		India

© Peter Cheverton and Jan Paul van der Velde, 2011

ISBN   978 0 7494 6123 2
E-ISBN 978 0 7494 6147 8

British Library Cataloguing-in-Publication Data

A CIP record for this book is available from the British Library.

Library of Congress Cataloging-in-Publication Data

Cheverton, Peter.
    Understanding the professional buyer : what every sales professional should know about how the modern buyer thinks and behaves / Peter Cheverton, Jan Paul van der Velde.
        p. cm.
    Includes bibliographical references and index.
    ISBN 978-0-7494-6123-2 – ISBN 978-0-7494-6147-8 (ebook)   1. Purchasing.
2. Selling.   3. Selling–Psychological aspects.   I. Velde, Jan Paul van der.   II. Title.
    HF5437.C52 2011
    658.8′04–dc22

                                                                                2010022265

Typeset by Graphicraft Limited, Hong Kong
Printed and bound in India by Replika Press Pvt Ltd
Printed using inks and consumables from Flint Group

Contents

Preface

This is a book about how buyers think and behave. That is not to say that they are always right in how they think and what they do, any more than salespeople, but it is as well to know what makes them tick.

The book is the work of two authors: one by background and experience a buyer (Jan Paul), the other a seller (Peter). Jan Paul tells it how it is, and we both took the decision at an early stage to keep it that way. We have not colluded on Jan Paul's text; the bulk of the book remains the unexpurgated view of a buyer (and a Dutch buyer at that, which many would say is the highest expression of the art . . .). You will not find in his words any mealy-mouthed compromises intended to keep both sides happy, but rather a completely honest account of how the buyer sees the world, and the expectations that result from that view. Where salespeople see the world in the same way (and Jan Paul repeatedly urges that they should try harder to do just that), then something approaching a happy partnership can be the result. Where salespeople refuse to recognize the buyer's perspective, then they can only have themselves to blame if the outcome is uncomfortable.

That is not to say that sellers should always take whatever is said lying down; recognizing a perspective is not the same as agreeing with it. At the end of each chapter Peter has inserted what we have called the *seller's response* – 'what might sales professionals make of what has been said, and how might they respond?' These sections have been written so as to stand alone, if that is how you wish to use them (no buyer has tampered with the words!), but it is strongly recommended that you read them in parallel with the buyer's text – this is after all a relationship of two perspectives.

Two perspectives, but only one outcome. In such cases the more that can be known about both perspectives, the more likely is an outcome that will please. That is the overriding purpose and intent of this book.

The seller's introduction

The seller–buyer relationship has endured for centuries, largely because it works, and that is largely because it is a relationship of equals – both have needs, both have ambitions, both have jobs to be done. Circumstances can of course disturb the balance of power and an unequal relationship can develop for a period of time – a buyer's market or a seller's market – but when both sides know that this is but a temporary affair, any abuses are mitigated by the knowledge that times will change and the boot may soon be on the other foot. Such are the checks and balances of the seller–buyer relationship.

Technology has played its part in determining the nature of the relationship, and it might be useful to mention just two examples. First, the motor car. Once sales professionals could travel beyond the same business community as their customer they began to acquire a new status (if they were smart enough to realize it): that of an expert. By broadening their horizons – seeing other customers working in different circumstances – they began to be of greater use, and interest, to their original customers. This gave them power and influence, against which buyers might protect themselves with tactics and stratagems. We have all played such games.

If the motor car conferred advantage on the seller (the buyers used theirs simply to get to work and back), the computer has done very much the reverse. While sales teams might use computers to design ever more impressive presentations, or to build sales monitoring systems worthy of Big Brother, buyers use them to measure supplier effectiveness, and we all know where that leads in the negotiating balance of power.

Of course, the motor car was the revolutionary technology of the last century, and the computer of this century, and that should be of concern to any sales professional. Over the last 10 years the balance of power between supplier and customer has shifted very much in the buyer's favour, and to a large extent simply because the buyer has better knowledge of what is going on between the two businesses.

One purpose of this book is to help redress that balance, because an equilibrium always makes for a healthier business relationship.

The buyer's introduction

Since I have been a purchasing professional for over 20 years, and for a number of years now have run, alongside my real job, sales and key account workshops with Insight Marketing and People,* I have had the opportunity

* See Chapter 14 for further details.

to meet a significant number of different salespeople operating in different industries and markets. It has never ceased to amaze me that, with a few exceptions, most salespeople do not seem to have a real understanding of what the buying profession is about. Not only is this strange (as the buyer is their counterpart in many commercial dealings), in fact it is pretty irresponsible to allow salespeople to visit buyers without understanding their processes, analyses and tactics. The lack of this knowledge will certainly damage the outcome of the sales–buyer interactions, I believe predominantly from a sales point of view.

Salespeople (whether we call them account managers, sales representatives, customer relationship managers or any other expensive fancy title) can in my eyes only be successful if, among other things, they understand the other side of the commercial table. While all sales courses talk about 'understanding the needs of the customer', 'focusing on the customer', 'listening to the customer' and other phrases along similar lines, the whole sales execution process almost seems to ignore the fact that the buyer is nowadays in many cases a key element in that customer process.

In an increasing number of companies purchasing professionals have moved into solid positions, and this development will continue. They are often the 'gateway' into the company, with quite far-reaching powers over purchasing decisions and even some decisions beyond the purely traditional purchasing remit. As a consequence they are in a position to exert significant backwards pressure on sales professionals across their entire commercial and technical agenda.

I know there are still people in sales who believe that 'the only good buyer is a dead one', or that 'the best way to work with a buyer is to avoid them'. However, these dinosaurs in sales are a dying species as they have proven to be less and less successful. Clearly it is still very important to influence not only the buyer but also other major stakeholders (as that influences the buyer subsequently internally); however, not understanding what drives the buyer leads to a high risk of not successfully closing the deal as the buyer regularly holds the ultimate contracting power – or could, at least, make the life of a salesperson difficult.

So why is it that salespeople, with all their skills, training programmes and the attention of their own senior management, are so unaware of the purchasing processes and the motivations of buyers that they have only a limited awareness of new developments in the purchasing area, and still believe they can do a good job? Do they believe that professional purchasing functions are temporary and that the old days of purchasing being an administrative function will come back? Do they think that managing buyers by ignoring their processes will help their own margins turn upwards again?

I believe one of the reasons is that, while purchasing as a function has started to develop quite fast in the last 15 years, the sales side has not been able to catch up and incorporate these changes into its processes and approaches. As a consequence companies still operate old-fashioned sales processes driven by 'innocent' sales representatives, whom they send to a group of purchasing professionals who are capable of eating them alive. But still we expect the sales professionals to do an excellent job. Are we surprised that some salespeople now think the only way a price can go is down?

The ignorance within the sales function (and the ignorance from management in general in most companies) of the buyers' processes, their insights, analyses and tactics, destroys enormous value in the sales process. It is also the main reason that on Friday afternoons when salespeople meet in the local pub, they share their horror stories of the 'awful buyers' who never seem to do what they are expected to.

Some people might conclude from this book that the purchasing side in all companies is now very much developed to world-class level, and that all buyers' decisions and actions are fully rational and understandable. I need to clear away that potential misperception. Obviously while the buying function has progressed significantly in general, buying Neanderthals do still exist. Indeed some of their tactics and approaches are awful, and destructive to the opportunity for the buying company to create value. Unfortunately there are still a lot of 'willing amateurs' who have major buying responsibilities without a full insight into and understanding of modern techniques. I am ashamed of this as a buying professional, but more important, I would ask their senior managers and company owners why they would allow a group of people to destroy value. But even so, if salespeople have some insight into these amateurs, their internal buying challenges, processes and analyses, they will stand a better chance, as they will be able to counter the buyers' arguments a lot better.

The buying function is undoubtedly changing, and a new breed of purchasing professionals have been trained and exposed to new tools, processes and analyses like the ones described in this book. More and more companies and public organizations are starting, or continuing, to invest in their purchasing staff. So if your customer has not yet reached the functional levels described here, you should be prepared for the time when they will.

Inevitably during my career I have been a purchasing professional in only a few industries and markets, but from the workshops I have carried out with Insight People and Marketing, I have been able to confirm that the basics apply to all industries and markets. This book does not aim to give a complete overview of all purchasing tactics, analyses and tools: there are too many. Furthermore, while it works through a number of key tools, it does not try to provide a theoretical or academic analysis of them. The focus is on how buyers use them in practice.

As a consequence the book should give you a good overview of thinking processes within the buying community. Certainly not all analysis techniques, tools and tactics are used in all industries, and certain industries carry out specific types of analysis on top of what is described in this book, but if you apply the tools and analysis discussed in this book to your own market and customers, it will undoubtedly give you a better understanding of their own value delivery process. In short, it is a route to working more effectively with buyers.

I am sure that the subjects and analyses in this book will trigger discussions within your company on the real sales value you offer, as they do in the workshops, and how you can best deliver it to customers. At a minimum, if buyers continue to act irrationally (in your eyes), and use leveraging tactics with which of course you disagree (because your product is obviously *very special*), it will enable you to ask some *hard* questions about the products and their marketing. In the end the perceptions of buyers, if generally applied in the market, are or will become reality for your products.

There is no risk that reading this book will turn you from a seller into a buyer. But it should give you a much better sense of your own position in relation to buyers, and of how you could work effectively with buyers for your own benefit.

Of course you might indeed be a buyer, and still be reading this book (probably only if you got it for free!). You might ask yourself why I have decided to share the tricks of the trade. I truly believe that the game will be much more rewarding in all its aspects if sales and buying personnel understand each other better. And I'm sure that there will be enough innocent salespeople left to let us still have a bit of the *old fun*.

And for Peter's '*seller's response*' comments, I forgive him; he is more a sales type anyway.

The Seller – Peter Cheverton
The Buyer – Jan Paul van der Velde

About the authors

Jan Paul van der Velde

After studying mechanical engineering, Jan Paul van der Velde (1964, Haarlem, The Netherlands) has had a career of over 20 years in purchasing. His career started at Philips Electronics as part of the purchasing trainee programme. After a few years Jan Paul moved to Frito Lay (PepsiCo), the leading global snack company, where he held several major purchasing roles including European Supply Chain Management. After 10 years at Frito Lay, his next position was at Heineken, the famous Dutch beer brewer, heading up the global packaging purchasing department, followed by six years at ICI/Quest International, a leading flavour and fragrance company, where he was responsible at management team level for the entire purchasing agenda. Currently he works at Flint Group, the leading provider of consumables to the printing and packaging industry worldwide, as SVP Procurement and part of the Executive Management Team.

In cooperation with INSIGHT Marketing and People, over the last 10 years Jan Paul has shared his experience in purchasing with sales/account executives through key account management/global account management master classes and specific in-house 'Purchasing for Salespeople' programmes. Many sales professionals have discovered that they thought they knew it all, but there was one thing about which they had little idea: what buyers were thinking and doing.

Peter Cheverton

Peter Cheverton is a founding Director of INSIGHT Marketing and People, a global training and consultancy firm specializing in key and global account management. He has developed an international reputation as one of the leading experts in this challenging area, working 'hands on' with clients in Europe, the Americas, AsiaPacific and Africa.

He is also the author of *Key Account Management* (4th edition), *Global Account Management*, *Key Account Management in Financial Services*, *Key Marketing Skills* (2nd edition), *Understanding Brands*, and *Building the Value Machine*.

Peter spends most of his time helping clients with the implementation of KAM strategies, and regularly presents INSIGHT's Key Account Management Masterclass around the world.

For contact details please see Chapter 14.

Acknowledgements

Jan Paul would like to thank his colleagues at Quest International, and especially Ali Armitage and Arno de Groot who have given constructive feedback, kept him focused on the key purchasing messages, and ensured the functional content was correct.

Peter Cheverton would like to thank his clients for allowing him to assess how well their sales professionals match up to the demands of the modern buyer, and for engaging him to help enhance those relationships.

Our most important inspiration, however, has been the many sellers and buyers we have observed over many years. Many of the examples in this book come straight from them and their experiences. You might even recognize yourself; those will be the good examples of course, while the less flattering stories will doubtless relate to other people...

1 Terminology

The purchasing function has developed relatively recently, so some of the terms used in this book need some explanation.

Even simple terms like buyer have evolved over time. As in many professions there is a consistent inflation of titles. We don't call sales people 'sellers' any more, but give them a fancy title like 'key account and customer relationship executive'. Buyers are competitive by nature, so the same is true for them.

In the context of this book, *buyers* refers to people who execute strategic processes for acquiring materials and services, irrespective of the title on their business card. These strategic processes include specifying, sourcing, negotiating, contracting and evaluating. In European literature this set of processes is normally referred to as *Purchasing*. The related operational processes of planning, making, moving, administration and control are frequently referred to in European literature as *Procurement*. In some companies these two very separate functions, which have quite distinct skill sets, are combined, but in world-class procurement organizations they tend to be split. The operational processes are mostly integrated with the operations function. This is sometimes referred to as the *supply chain*, but that is not entirely correct, because the strategic processes of purchasing also need to be part of the extended supply chain process.

To make the matter more complicated, in the rest of the world the two terms are frequently reversed, with procurement being used for the strategic functions, and purchasing for the operational ones. We have decided to use the European definitions, but you should keep in mind that our focus is on the strategic processes.

Job titles often found in this strategic area include: strategic sourcing manager, inbound supply chain manager (although this term is also used for the operational processes) and purchasing manager. Add to that the different levels in the organization by changing the word manager for executive, director, (senior) vice-president (SVP/VP) or any other fancy title and we have made a reasonably complete overview of the different job titles used in the purchasing area.

Also for the purpose of this book, we introduce the term 'item' to represent both materials and services. At the generic level, in most cases everything that is valid for the purchasing of physical goods, whether they are raw materials to be used in production or operational supplies to be used in running the company (from paperclips to production equipment), is also valid for the procurement of services. 'Item' therefore could mean either a tangible good or a service.

The seller's response...

What can there be to say about definitions? Plenty, and vital stuff too. It matters greatly what you call your buyer, and for the simple reason that buyers have feelings, and ambitions, and pride, just like salespeople.

Perhaps you, as a seller, are not too keen on being referred to as a 'sales rep', or worse, a 'traveller' – your business card doubtless declares you as something rather grander than that. Well, make sure you don't cause the same offence by appearing to misjudge the buyer's task through inappropriate language. Lesson one of handling buyers (whatever they may call themselves): speak their language.

I realize that they do not always reciprocate. I'm sure you would rather that your vitally important 'value added solution' was not referred to as an 'item', but be patient. If you want them to change how they think about you and your offer, then it is usually best to start on their territory, and the words you use are important in this respect.

Much of the advice given throughout this book will have a common theme: matching. In order to match the buyer's expectations we must begin by matching their modes of work, including the nature of their analyses. In order to do this we must go back another step and start by matching their language. By doing this the seller begins to enter the world of the buyer, and at that point the clouds begin to clear.

2 Purchasing developments: what has changed

Ever since trade was invented, there have been sellers and buyers, but in contrast to the sales function, it took a long time before purchasing was seen as a real profession with an important strategic side to it, and not just an administrative support role. Even today, while its importance is fully recognized in most companies, many people cannot see that purchasing is at a similar strategic level to for example sales, marketing or product development. As a consequence they do not view purchasing as a real career opportunity.

Now let us look at the major changes in the purchasing function, and consider why salespeople need to be aware of them. Until the late 1980s and early 1990s there tended to be a lack of attention to purchasing in business education and training, but this then started to change, and business schools began to see opportunities in the purchasing process. From an economic logic viewpoint, it is surprising that it took so long. You might think it self-evident that managing buying wisely is critical to running an efficient organization: why did the academic, consultancy and business world not realize that sooner? Clearly in order to manage a sustainable and profitable company, it is not only important to manage the product portfolio, the selling prices and the internal costs, it is also crucial to manage the external spend professionally. Most companies spend a significant proportion of their turnover on directly or indirectly bought-in materials and services. Furthermore, with increased outsourcing and focus on key activities, the percentage of external spend will probably grow further in the future, so the relative importance of managing purchasing will increase.

The interest of the academic world resulted in an increased number of studies on purchasing, and the development of process models and all kinds of toolboxes. The most important ones are outlined in this book.

More recently, the introduction and widespread use of the internet has made a world of a difference to buyers. In the past they were more dependent on input from salespeople, but now they can get just about any information they need on the world wide web. So today's buyers have better insights into the market, and this puts them in a stronger positions, as knowledge influences the power balance. The internet has also enabled buying groups within the same company to share information more effectively, and this has brought them a better leverage potential. The internet has spelled the end of local and regional pricing, except where there are import restrictions in place. Yet how many companies price their offerings differently in different regions, and then are surprised when global buyers start to take advantage of that?

Different industry sectors have adopted new purchasing techniques and tools at different rates. Industries with a relatively high percentage of external spend or with significant margin challenges, such as expensive consumer goods (cars, electronics and so on) were the front-runners in improving their purchasing processes. Companies like Toyota and Honda of America are regularly quoted as the leaders. The well-known purchasing initiatives at General Motors/Volkswagen (under the leadership of Jose Ignacio Lopez) are also seen as a landmark in the trend to pay increased attention to the function, even though the jury is still out on whether these destroyed or created value, but without doubt they created enough attention to start a change process.

Companies in most industries have now carried out purchasing initiatives, sometimes quite publicly, with quarterly updates on their progress as part of their shareholder communications; others have taken similar initiatives in a more low-key manner, although this did not mean they were less well supported by general management. As purchasing leverage and synergies clearly became hot topics in boardrooms, most consultancy firms developed purchasing and sourcing excellence programmes, and a number of purchasing benchmarks are now available.

Probably the most recent buyers to start adopting new purchasing techniques are those in the public sector. These include buyers for a wide range of publicly funded activities, including physical infrastructure, education and healthcare. Although they have adopted the types of strategy outlined in this book, they have several additional challenges, not least a wider range of key stakeholders, including politicians, who tend to make the buying decision more difficult by making public statements and adding demands to the specifications. Further, the numerous rules that governments put in place on how to grant major contracts also limit the full buying potential. However, those rules are arguably a logical trade-off against transparency, which affects a government organization in a different way than it does a public or private company. In this book we do not focus specifically on these additional challenges facing government organizations, but clearly external influences on the buying decision in a government organization can be significantly greater than in a private or public company.

Following the increased interest in the academic and consultancy worlds in the purchasing function, a new breed of purchasing professionals started to emerge. Most national purchasing associations, which were traditionally responsible for the training of purchasing professionals, increased their efforts by upgrading their training programmes and bringing in more experts; this was the case, for example, with the Chartered Institute of Purchasing and Supply (CIPS) in the United Kingdom, and the Institute for Supply Management (ISM) in the United States (all linked by the International Federation of Purchasing and Supply Management (IFPSM): for details of all national purchase organizations see www.ifpmm.org). A number of the associations also started to sponsor academic purchasing programmes, re- sulting in further functional developments. Now there are respected MBAs with a key focus on purchasing all around the world.

While it could still be argued that the purchasing function is under- represented at senior level in many organizations and that the tools and techniques are not yet shared in more general management programmes, it is clear that the function has gone through an enormous, irreversible development process, and that it is here to stay. On the other hand it must be said that senior executives in most executive management teams still underestimate the value that good buyers can deliver, not just in reducing overheads, but also by contributing to margin management, the innovation agenda, low-cost operation, in- and outsourcing, and more generically to developing effective and efficient supply chains. Not infrequently in internal reviews, operations and establishment costs are reviewed to the nth degree and then there is just one short paragraph on developments in raw material costs, even though the costs of raw materials could be four or five times higher than the operational costs.

The new buyers are no longer 'administrators' who convert an internal requisition into an external purchase order and perhaps do some price bar- gaining in between the administrative processes. They are developing to be well-trained strong individuals, who can communicate at all levels of man- agement and think cross-functionally. They have the ability to understand the dynamics of the markets in which they operate, and have a good general knowledge of the products and service they buy. They understand internal and external stakeholders, and are capable of developing well-articulated sourcing strategies. In an increasing number of companies, purchasing has been upgraded to board level, with a *chief purchasing officer* (CPO), or operates just under the board in the key operational management teams.

With all these changes happening over a time span of two decades, it is clear that a *purchasing revolution* has taken place. Clearly this means that purchasing makes a major contribution to managing a sustainable profitable company. Purchasing is too important to leave to 'willing amateurs' or administrators. *This should therefore also mean that the way that sales processes were run 20 years ago and the way they should be run now should be quite different.*

Surprisingly, however, it looks as if the sales side has not noticed the upgrade of the purchasing function, or at least has not taken sufficient action to adapt to the new situation. In order to be successful it is critical that salespeople understand the new situation and can 'read' the minds of their commercial counterparts, so that they can work with buyers and ensure that they are using the right selling strategies and tactics.

This book tries to fill part of that knowledge gap by describing in a simple way the processes, analyses, toolboxes and purchasing themes currently used by buying professionals. It also provides some hints, tips and tricks for improving the offering of products to customers via professional buyers.

The seller's response...

The message is clear: sellers need to catch up, and this book is written as a wake-up call. It is true that the buyer's world has changed more dramatically than that of the seller, and that this has caused something of a tilt to the once level (though it might never have seemed so!) playing field.

In many cases this imbalance has led to suppliers seeing their value eroded, even denied, and in the most dramatic of cases they have suffered what we might call a complete value meltdown. There will have been many and various reasons for this, but a significant one, and an avoidable one, will have been the supplier's inability to understand the buyer's agenda. Suppliers that know they will be working against the buyer's agenda can at least prepare themselves for the opposition they will encounter, but a supplier that is in ignorance of that agenda is in danger of sleep-walking into the relationship, and is very likely to be surprised by the actions taken against it. This is the road to value erosion.

If you have suffered such value erosion (I hope not meltdown!), then reading this book is intended to prevent such somnambulism and help you find a new and proper equilibrium with the buyer. If you have not suffered, then reading this book may just help you keep it that way!

There is another message in this chapter, one that is less strident (perhaps not surprisingly when we consider its honesty): buyers often feel unloved. Jan Paul says 'underestimated', but he means much the same thing, that many buyers feel unloved (or underestimated) by their own business colleagues and senior managers. Think hard about what this means to you as the supplier.

Do you see it as a cause for celebration? Perhaps it demonstrates what you, as the seller, always suspected: that the buyers are not as powerful as they like to suggest? Perhaps it suggests that the best course of action is to go around them, to find the people that really matter? Perhaps it does, and many have taken such a line, but might there be a better approach?

It is often true that buyers are not as powerful as they suggest, but is that any reason to make an enemy of them? How powerful might they prove to be *as a thorn in your flesh*?

If having a buyer as an opponent is a bad thing, then how about having buyers so unimportant within their own organization that no reliance can be put on their word? This can be just as bad, perhaps worse – at least you know where you stand when the buyer is just plain against you!

The savvy seller plays a smarter game. By all means make contacts with those beyond the buyer, but never do so without the buyer's knowledge, or without the buyer's permission. Better still, do it with the buyer's help and active participation, aiming at all points to raise their status and position as you proceed. The seller who can win buyers the internal recognition they so clearly desire is a seller who will succeed on many other fronts. Moreover, sellers who can help establish their buyers as an important part of the decision-making process are sellers who have gone some way to making *themselves* a part of that same decision-making process – an enviable position for any supplier to hold.

It may surprise you to learn that some buyers do not in fact seek power. With power comes responsibility, and that can be a problem. The buyer lives a pressured enough life – bad buying decisions can have a devastating effect on their own business, far more so than a bad job done by a seller – and many buyers seek to reduce that pressure, not see it increase.

The surest way to increase the pressure on buyers is to let them down. Most buyers usually discount the promises made by suppliers by a good 20 per cent, precisely in anticipation of such let-downs, as a way of protecting themselves from the criticisms of their own colleagues. The supplier will do well to understand where those internal criticisms are most likely to arise, and take actions to reduce or eliminate them. Perhaps the buyer works on behalf of multiple sites, and one of those sites is always complaining about poor service, late deliveries, variable quality and the like. That site may receive no worse service from the supplier than any of the others, but it is the one that shouts loudest, and it is the one that raises the buyer's pressure gauge. The supplier's task is obvious in such a case I hope: make sure that site gets first-class attention, and make sure the buyer knows it.

I have been told by many buyers (though not at the time I have been negotiating with them) that price is almost never their biggest worry. One said to me that buyers were never 'kicked up the backside' by their bosses or colleagues over a price deal, but were often chastised when a supplier let them down over an issue of service or quality. Mark these comments well. Their colleagues, let's say in the production department, will rarely know what price the buyer has negotiated, but they certainly notice if the product arrives late or does not meet specifications. The moral of the story is clear: if you ensure that service and quality issues are attended to, and if that means the buyers have a less pressured life within their own organization, then you might expect to see a reward for your efforts, by way of price.

The real trick to this equation is not simply that you ensure perfect service and quality, but that you ensure buyers *know the effort* you have put into achieving this, and achieving it on their behalf.

3 The importance of purchasing for a company

It is only in the last couple of decades that people have begun to focus upon the importance of a professional and strategic purchasing process. So why have we seen companies paying increased attention to the purchasing agenda?

There is one simple cause: purchasing results have a significant effect on the bottom line, for two reasons. One is the obvious one: the costs of the items purchased. The other is related to supply chain flexibility and the innovation agenda.

While costs have an immediate effect on the bottom line, the longer-term effect is more important. Costs have an effect not only on the margin but also on the top line, as it is crucial for a company to have *controlled cost levels*; in many cases it is vital to have lower cost levels than one's competitors. Of course, this does not mean that companies should *just* have a cost focus: having the right products or services, creating the right value or being able to create a market are all key aspects of a successful business. However, with markets becoming more global and more transparent, a company cannot survive in the long term if its costs (both internal and external) are either uncontrolled or in the long term are significantly higher than those of its direct competitors. This price pressure exists throughout the supply chain, from consumers to producers of raw materials and service providers. At each step of the chain, the company needs to ensure that it stays competitive, which means costs must be similar to or better than its competitors'; part of the cost pressure needs to be funnelled through to the suppliers.

In most companies, purchases represent a significant proportion of turn-over, and the trend towards outsourcing means that this percentage is likely to increase. If we consider a typical company's profit and loss account, it very quickly becomes evident that, for purely economic reasons, it is critical to manage external costs.

Even in industries where the costs of raw materials appear to be less dominant, such as pharmaceuticals, why do the major companies struggle to compete with low-priced generics? Arguably it is because when a drug is first patented the raw material costs look unimportant, but when the patent expires and does not give price protection any more, those costs suddenly become important – but then it is too late to start managing them.

There are several ways to look at the effect of purchasing on company results. First of all we shall look at the direct profit and loss (P&L) effect. It is apparent from the balance sheet that external spend in many cases is signi-ficant, and therefore should be managed carefully and should have a direct link to overall margin management to ensure the company's ongoing pro-fitability. Second, we shall look at the effect that purchasing has on the return on investment (RoI), using the DuPont Return on Investment model.

From the late 1990s to the first years of the new century, in many industries purchasing went through a period of almost over-focus, frequently referred to as the '*purchasing tiger*' period. This led to a number of major changes in the ways that companies ran their purchasing processes and aligned their purchasing organizations. As with all things that are subject to an 'over-focus', the attention on purchasing is now returning to normal levels, but it remains significantly higher than it was before 1990.

Understanding the importance of the purchasing process and its financial impact on the buying company is beneficial, even crucial, for salespeople. It enables them to understand why buying companies take certain actions and react strongly to competitive pressures in their sourcing.

The economic logic: purchasing's effect on the bottom line

To understand the effect of purchasing prices on the P&L account, we can take a very simple generic example. Our business's P&L account looks like this:

Sales	100
Raw materials & other third-party spend	60
Personnel	20
Other	10
Profit	10

Now let's assume that market forces oblige the company to lower its sales price across the board by 5 per cent. To keep things simple, we assume all costs vary with volumes, which is obviously not entirely true. The new P&L would look like this:

Sales	**95**
Raw materials & other third-party spend	**60**
Personnel	**20**
Other	**10**
Profit	**5**

This 5 per cent reduction in selling prices leads to a 50 per cent reduction in profits. We can safely assume that most companies would not regard that as acceptable, so action needs to be taken to restore profits to a reasonable level. In order to get the profit back up to 10 per cent of turnover, the company could:

- double its sales;
- reduce its personnel by 25 per cent;

OR

- find 8.3 per cent of purchasing savings.

Doubling the sales is unlikely to be possible in the short term. If overall demand was there to do it, why would you have had to lower your sales price by 5 per cent to start with. Nor is it very realistic to suppose the company could produce the same output with 25 per cent fewer people, at least without making major investments or structural changes. But finding purchasing savings of up to 8.3 per cent not only sounds feasible but would also have the fewest negative internal effects. Basically, it means that the suppliers of this company would need to pick up the bill for the agreed 5 per cent price reduction on the sales side.

This example is too simple to use for an in-depth analysis, but it enables us to make some very clear points. First, many salespeople are not really aware that a reduction in selling price has a disproportionately large impact on profits. Buyers often try to persuade salespeople to reduce their prices by holding out the carrot of an increased sales volume. However, as the example shows, it takes a very big increase in volume to make up for a comparatively small price reduction.

In accounting terms, if we continue to assume that all costs are variable, the situation is even worse than our simple arithmetic above suggests. If you were to double your sales volume after a 5 per cent price cut, and therefore make the same *amount* of profit, it would still mean that your *percentage* profit (compared with turnover) had halved. The entire company has had to make all that additional effort to double the sales, and for no more profit! And it's a big assumption that doubling turnover would mean a return to the original profit figure: that depends on how the additional activity affects the company's costs; for example did you have the capacity to double your production in the first place? Perhaps a part of the reduction in the sales price will be 'earned back' by an increase in volume, but only if all other costs do not increase proportionately (as might be the case with personnel and probably part of the third-party spend). So in general it is a very bad idea to agree to a significant reduction in selling price, even to obtain some increase in volume, as it will hit the bottom line very hard.

However, companies do regularly reduce the selling prices, for all kinds of reasons. These include a competitive market environment, underutilization of assets, and a desire for top-line growth (with margin reduction throughout). But salespeople need to recognize that they should always explain the exact reason why they are able to offer a price reduction, otherwise there is a significant risk that the buyer is likely to conclude that the original price was too high. This leads to buyers thinking that there is always an 'inflated' element in the first price they are quoted, and that they need to try for a reduction for no other reason than 'I assume you have built in inflation.'

It is easy to conclude from our analysis that every time a company reduces its selling prices, it should pass to its purchasers the challenge of recouping the losses from suppliers. Compared with other ways of saving money, as we saw above, the numbers tend to look quite feasible. But after doing this a few times, a buyer is likely to encounter the law of diminishing returns. Purchasing people could already hear the echo of pressure from internal salespeople: 'It's only 8.3 per cent. You should see what our customers' purchasing teams are doing to us!' In addition this encourages buyers to focus purely on price, especially if their target and bonus arrangements are geared towards just this. A pure price focus is very likely to destroy value for the buying company over time, as will be explained later in the book.

Purchasing importance: the DuPont RoI model

A simple P&L account, as described above, provides a good feel for the effect of price changes, both on the selling and on the buying side, but the DuPont chart (outlined in Figure 3.1) provides a better way of looking at purchasing's effects on the success (or better to say value) of a company. It links turnover speed to earnings as a percentage of sales, and enables us to see the effect of changes in costs, sales or level of investment.

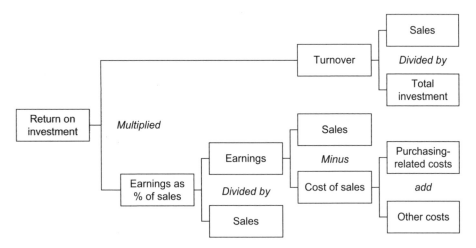

Figure 3.1   The DuPont return on investment chart

One of the standard measures of the success of a company is its return on investment. As defined here, RoI takes profit as a percentage of sales (in other words, it divides the amount of profit by the total sales figure) then multiplies that by the turnover. This leads to two figures: one that indicates the speed of the return, and another that gives the level of the return. Together they show how well an investment has been repaid. The higher either figure is (that is, the more rapid the return, or the higher it is overall), the more attractive this company is to invest in. This is regarded as the 'value' of the company.

We can show an example by using the data we used in the simplified P&L model, and adding to it to indicate additional costs, sales and investments:

- sales of 100;
- investment of 50;
- earnings of 5 (= 5 per cent);
- approximately 60 per cent of the overall costs are purchasing related.

Putting these figures into the DuPont model gives us Figure 3.2.

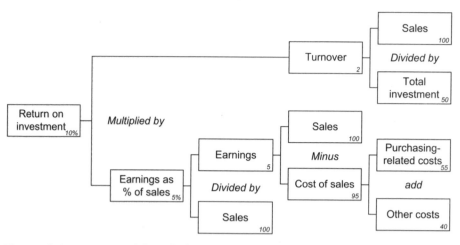

Figure 3.2 DuPont model – calculation example 1

Now let's assume that this company decides it needs a more proactive and professional approach towards its purchasing. Benchmarks based on years of experience in many industries show that if categories of spend have not been managed professionally in the past, improving their management leads typically to savings in the double-digit range. For this example however, we shall assume that the new professional purchasing function achieves a small price reduction of 5 per cent across the board, with all other aspects of the company's operations remaining the same. Figure 3.3 shows the revised model.

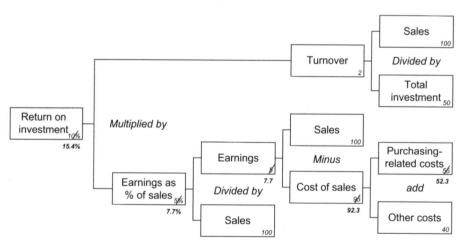

Figure 3.3 DuPont model – calculation example 2

The outcome is amazing. A 5 per cent reduction in purchase prices leads to a 54 per cent improvement in return on investment. To put this a different way, if other costs move in proportion to sales (more probably the movement will be slightly less than linear) and purchasing-related costs move linearly (which for direct spend is probably right, but for indirect it will again be slightly below linear), there would need to be an increase in sales of over 50 per cent to reach the same improvement in RoI. And this is only true if the level of investment does not go up to facilitate that sales increase; otherwise the improvement that comes from reducing purchasing-related costs is unlikely to be achieved by any sales increase.

So we can see very clearly what effect purchase prices have on the bottom line and on the RoI in a company. In this example, of course, we have looked at a price reduction; clearly a price increase has the opposite, negative, effect.

Salespeople should therefore not be so surprised that buyers (and their management teams in the background) fight so hard against price increases. Salespeople find it hard to push through price increases not just because buyers want to get a good bargain or to protect their bonus, but because buyers understand what a massive effect purchase price increases can have on the company's competitive position. It is part of their job to work to keep prices low, both because the impact shows up immediately in the profit margin, and because in the longer term it affects the RoI, and thus the attractiveness of the company to investors.

Companies typically struggle to protect their bottom line in the face of raw material price fluctuations. It is hard to pass purchase price increases through to end customers, either partially or in full. Even when the company does so, there normally is a significant time lag between the purchase price increase and the sales price increase that is intended to compensate for it. Buyers understand this, and know that if they accept an increase, their company's results are likely to suffer. They also will struggle to pass this on into the market, so the company's margin will take a hit, at least for the time-lag period. Second, they also know that if they can negotiate a decrease in purchase prices, even if this is linked to general downward market movements, this will enhance the margin, because there is likely to be the same time lag before this passes through to sales price reductions to their own customers. Good buyers therefore need to be on top of market weaknesses, so they can quickly capture the opportunity to negotiate a price decrease, and will use delaying tactics if the market is firming up, maximizing the benefits of the general time lag.

These two analyses of the effects of purchase prices on company results help to explain why companies are increasingly paying significant and ongoing attention to the buying function. However, while buyers understand and make use of this strong financial rationale, the pricing logic always helps the establishment of a good purchasing environment. Despite the strength of the immediate financial rationale, world-class buyers will be careful in over-emphasizing this, because it tends to undermine the other main areas in which a good purchasing organization can contribute to the company. By following only the financial rationale in negotiations, buyers may give the impression that costs are the only thing that matters, which is certainly not the case.

Since the economic argument is so overwhelming, both buyers and sales-people face a real challenge to ensure that other elements of the purchasing agenda, such as value creation, innovation and security of supply, are not overshadowed. Buyers and salespeople do in fact have a common interest in ensuring that these elements are managed alongside the pricing/cost agenda. If the focus is wider than just price, and the negotiations are multidimensional, the chance that agreements will reflect a better 'win–win' situation will increase significantly.

This therefore represents an opportunity for salespeople. However, this opportunity is not often embraced. If you can align yourself with the buyers' agenda on other aspects of the commercial relationship, you have the chance to construct a good buyers' 'internal sales story'. This alignment will help both the buyer and potentially your own sales position. However, do not kid yourself that the commercial pressure to keep costs down will disappear. Pricing is just too important to the success of your customer's organization; there is no way they can let the price/cost debate slip. What's more, it's in your interest as a seller to keep costs on the agenda: if your customer becomes more uncompetitive, what will happen to your sales volumes?

The rise and fall of purchasing: what next?

In the last 5 to 10 years, the buying functions of major companies have un-doubtedly gained power within their own organizations. In some companies this power took quite an extreme form, which is frequently referred to as the 'rise of the purchasing tiger'. Why did this happen, and will it disappear again? Will the purchase decision be returned to the end-user, or has the model changed once and for all?

There were several drivers for the rise of the purchasing tiger. After the economic growth in the late 1990s, mainly driven by internet/millennium activities, an economic slowdown hit most markets. Companies had got used to showing improved results each quarter that were originally driven by volume growth levels, and in achieving these many had failed to properly monitor their costs. If they were to continue to build (or rebuild) shareholder value, and to maintain their improved results, most markets and companies had to move into some level of cost management, as improvements were no longer supported by volume growth. The external spend is a predominant factor in many industries, so increased attention to buying was a logical move. At the same time there was a move towards strategic developments and approaches in purchasing, partly driven by the main consultancy groups. These attracted management attention, and purchasing moved into the spotlight.

Supported by the highest levels of management, many companies started to invest in their purchasing teams by pulling in talent, and seeking support and advice from major consultancy companies to help them upgrade the processes and organizational set-up. Owing to the support from the top, it was suddenly possible to take the kinds of major steps that had previously not been possible because of the lack of buy-in. Purchasing decisions were moved away from the end-users into newly formed or upgraded buying organizations. Item rationalization was suddenly purchasing led, and technical functions were needed to support these initiatives with significant resources.

In most cases these moves generated quick wins and quick cash. All this coincided with the e-procurement hype, and in a number of companies purchasing became almost untouchable.

Such a revolution obviously generates problems. First, it was not easy to find skilled procurement people, and although most companies could achieve some short-term savings, building a true strategy and a real approach towards sourcing, and thus obtaining long-term benefits, requires more than just building leverage and bidding via the internet. Running a successful company is not just about running the purchasing processes well, and some of the purchasing trends that were seen in the first decade of the 21st century were over the top. In trying to make their purchasing function strong, some companies arguably overshot in their approach. By focusing on gaining savings through core listing activities, auctioning, rapid and aggressive supplier switches and so on, they caused significant problems elsewhere: in innovation, quality and reliability, for example.

Without the right product (and this includes innovation) and the right sales process (including the right mix of customers and the right marketing methods), there is no company. There has to be a balance. Historically many people have said that unless a company has the right product and succeeds in generating sales, it is irrelevant what it pays for sourced items, hence the limited attention paid to the buying processes. The principle is correct: no buying is required if there are no sales; but on the other hand, a sustainable, ongoing, healthy company must have a long-term, sustainable, competitive purchasing process. Ongoing price pressure is essential for the health of the buying company, and salespeople will therefore continue to see pressure to cut costs and/or make product improvements.

The overall balance between innovation, security of supply, quality and diversification needs to be considered. Where previously purchasing had been under-represented, it was also not sustainable for it to be over-represented, and most companies have moved back to a more balanced approach to the overall sourcing and purchasing agenda. But one thing these years proved was the value of well-managed sourcing activities. As a consequence, buying's influence will not go away because its impact on the success of a company has become so evident.

Between 2003 and mid-2008 the rationale for a more balanced approach to inbound sourcing became very clear, as many companies faced challenges caused by supply security problems and rapidly increasing prices. Over the previous 10 to 15 years most markets had been geared to ever-reducing purchase prices, but now many companies had to announce that they faced challenges to their bottom line as a result of 'raw material price increases that could not be passed on with the same speed to the customer base'. An increased number of companies also faced serious service issues caused by problems with the availability of raw materials. In previous years, of course, individual items had changed in price, which could affect a conglomerate's product portfolio or a specific industry, but now most markets and industries faced challenges across the board at a level they had not seen before.

A number of factors served to exacerbate the shortages and sudden changes in demand and supply, including a sharp increase in oil prices, a massive growth in demand in Asia, a number of crop challenges, and weather-related issues. Most companies had been running in 'cost-savings mode', with a significant focus on keeping cash flow tight (and making improvements each quarter), and were used to constantly reducing prices, so they were running light on stocks. The entire inbound chain was therefore critically exposed to any changes farther up the chain, and a significant number of inbound challenges arose at the same time.

Suddenly, purchasing was less about savings, but more about managing increases and risks, and securing inbound supplies. However, a number of companies had lost what had been important supplier relationships and building back a secure inbound network takes time.

Then in mid-2008, when companies had just learned the new game of managing shortages, price increases and support margin management, suddenly the markets started to fall even more rapidly than they had risen previously. The tightening of the markets that had happened over a period of two to four years was reversed in six to eight months. The crisis that hit worldwide economies, starting as a financial crisis but moving to encompass overall issues of trust, was followed by a major drop in global demand for almost all items and across all industries and regions. This created an enormous challenge for purchasing functions. Suddenly sales prices were under enormous downwards price pressure, stocks in the chain were high compared to the new buying volumes (and had a high cost, compared with their replacement value), and while from the outset it might have seemed that buyers were in the driving seat again, in fact managing such a free fall brought all kinds of challenges.

Companies that have survived these upward and downward trends have obviously learned valuable lessons from these challenges, on both the selling and the buying side. For the buying side it has become very apparent that price reductions will not continue for ever: prices depend on market forces, and tend to run in cycles. The last cycle ran for a quite a long time in one direction, but that did not mean that it could not be reversed. The same is true for the enormous and unprecedentedly fast fall of the markets more recently. This also showed that using leverage is not the only tactic, and that security of supply requires an ongoing effort. In short, buying organizations need to select the right strategies and tactics from a palette of alternatives, in order to manage all possible market circumstances, opportunities and risks. That palette had always been available to them, but 'economic laziness' meant that a whole generation of buyers had limited themselves to one tactic, using leverage and power plays. The recent upswing and sudden crash have provided a good, though expensive, lesson for buyers. With the recent challenges in mind, there is a good chance that purchasing departments will be able to persuade their senior managers of the need for strategic supplier and purchasing management, not just for price and costs savings (although those will still be important).

This represents an opportunity for the selling side to talk about subjects other than just pricing. Those customers who were worst hit in the past by security of supply challenges are more likely to discuss how to avoid such problems in the future. It also opens an opportunity to discuss price in a way that is based more on market facts and cost drivers. The opportunity for salespeople is created by the fact that buyers have realized that historically they have not been taking care of some of the buying fundamentals that drive the price/cost equation, and that these need to be managed to ensure a sustainable long-term situation. (These purchasing fundamentals are explained in Chapter 8 on purchasing analysis.)

The seller's response...

I hope that reading this chapter has given you an optimistic outlook on pricing. Buyers who look forward within their supply chain, perhaps seeking cost reductions within their own operations, as opposed to those who simply look backwards, seeking price reductions, are of course the answer to a long-spoken prayer.

Jan Paul makes quite clear the ambition of modern buyers to do just this; he goes further, counselling sellers not to fall into the trap of price reductions as the answer to all difficulties. Price reductions, in the long run, can be damaging to both sides, particularly if they lead to lower quality, reduced innovation, or increased risk to supplies. All of this is music to the ears of the 'added value' supplier, but this is no time for such suppliers to rest on their laurels.

The requirement is clear: if you are not going to reduce your prices, then make very sure that you act to reduce the customer's costs, or to improve their performance, or to reduce their risk, and so on. But even if you achieve any of those things, this is still not enough.

The seller must also aim to understand the often complex cause and effect models that operate within the customer's business, and understand them as well as the buyer, perhaps better. If suppliers seek to argue a case for higher prices based on some beneficial impact within the customer's business, then they must be able to speak the language of return on investment, and speak it in the same tone as the buyer. If you skipped over those (RoI) charts because they seemed rather daunting, go back and master them – it may prove to be one of the best returns on your own investment of time.

Of even greater importance, if you aim to increase your prices, then it is vital to start by understanding the impact on your customer's business. Price increases are never easy, but suppliers who arrive armed with arguments about their own rising costs are not exactly helping their cause. Price increases that come with some mitigating benefit – meaning something that makes a positive impact on the customer's issues – are more likely to succeed, particularly if the seller has done the necessary homework and can argue that the new benefits outweigh the new costs, on a return on investment basis.

The 'return' on the customer's investment does not always have to be to do with costs, as this chapter makes clear. The modern buyer is concerned with a balanced package that includes price at one end, but also includes risk management at the other. This is good news, but the seller has to do a little better than the hackneyed line: 'If you go for something cheaper you'll be sorry in the long run.' The seller needs to know the nature of the risk: exactly what will the implications to the customer's business be, of their being 'sorry in the long run'? Can they be quantified? Are you, the seller, able to measure them on the customer's behalf?

As well as having feelings, buyers are often quite lazy (they begin to sound almost human . . .) and will very much appreciate the supplier who spends time doing their work for them – provided of course they do it honestly. Don't expect to be rewarded (or even believed) for the all too common 'company brochure' style presentation of benefits, but you can expect to make progress if you take the time to translate these generalities into the specifics of the customer's business.

To measure value received on behalf of the customer it will often be necessary to get inside the customer's business – literally to get on to their shop floor – though you must take care not to be seen to be interfering in their operations, or seeking to have undue influence on the internal decision-making process. The best way to avoid such criticism is to have a 'specialist' from your own organization take on such tasks. Buyers are suspicious (often rightly) of sales people 'wandering around' their premises, but a specialist with a clear brief is more likely to be seen as 'helping' rather than 'interfering'.

4 Purchasing processes

If sales professionals are to work more effectively with purchasing people, it is important for them to understand the full purchasing process. Salespeople normally only see a small part of the entire process – the point at which the seller and buyer interact – and this might lead them to conclude that this is all there is to it. Not so: the entire purchasing process encompasses substantially more than this relatively straightforward commercial interaction. A salesperson who lacks understanding and insight into the entire process will undoubtedly miss opportunities to influence buying decisions. It is essential to understand the interaction between the buyer and other key stakeholders in the buying company. These interactions have major effects on how decisions are made, so a salesperson who can influence the processes should also be able to influence the buying decision – in their company's favour, naturally.

At a high level the purchasing process is quite simple. There is a requirement for an item, somebody searches for a supplier, a deal is done, and the item is delivered and paid for in a three-step administrative process involving a purchase order, invoice and receipt. However, this description of the buying process focuses only on the short-term transactional steps. Imagine describing the sales operation in terms of a customer ordering from a price list and the salesperson making sure that the item is then delivered and invoiced for. True, these steps are necessary, but no one would argue that this is what 'selling' is all about. This is just the admin; the skill comes in getting the sale.

Similarly, the administrative part of purchasing is necessary, but strategically and tactically trivial. The real meat comes in the process of determining (and influencing) what is required, selecting a supplier, determining the contracting strategies and tactics, commercial negotiations and contracting processes, contract implementation, contract follow-up and supplier evaluation. The whole thing is more challenging than it might have looked at first sight.

In this chapter we explain the purchasing process, starting with a quite simple 'silo' perspective, then considering a more detailed process, leading into a complete value chain model with a detailed description of purchasing activities, including drawing up a contract and closing the loop with contract follow-up. If salespeople understand the different processes better, they can create more opportunities to align with their customers and deliver value to them.

The basic purchasing process

There are many ways to look at the basic purchasing process. The simplest is to consider the different activities that ultimately lead to a contract. These are:

- Specify the requirement.
- Source: that is, find an item that meets the technical requirements from a supplier that meets the supplier requirements (see Chapter 8 on purchasing analysis for a discussion of supplier requirements).
- Negotiate: this is a process whereby terms and conditions are discussed and agreed.
- Contract: one of the two parties writes up the details of the negotiated agreement and the other agrees to the final text. This can be a formal legal process. Also part of the contracting process is internal communication (and administration) in both the seller and buyer companies.
- Contract follow-up: the process of evaluating what has been delivered against what had been agreed.

Figure 4.1 is a flow chart of these processes.

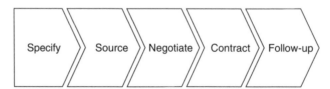

Figure 4.1 The basic procurement process

Now let us look at the activities in more detail.

The flow of events starts with the *specification process*. In more old-fashioned purchasing process descriptions, specification takes place before the purchasing function gets involved. Some people argue that the end-user specifies *what* the requirements are (in other words, draws up the product or service specification), while the buyer decides *where* to buy it from and on what terms and conditions. In theory this provides a clear-cut division of responsibilities, but the reality is a bit more complex. The choice of what to buy influences where it is bought and the final conditions. So there is a major benefit if the end-user and the buyer work closely together, iteratively refining the three aspects. This has a number of major benefits.

First of all, to a significant extent the specifications determine the costs of the item to be purchased. Take the simple example of buying a car. Specifying that it must be a large vehicle with a powerful engine not only means that it is likely to cost more to buy than a compact, small-engine car, it will also make a difference to the costs of using it. But both large and small cars have the same basic function: to move people from A to B. Would a lower-specification car be equally acceptable, or would a higher-specification car pay for itself (through faster journeys or increased reliability, say)? Careful thought needs to be given to issues such as these. Of course this is a very simple example, but it makes the point that determining the specification could have (and in most cases will have) major effects on the final purchase price and the total life cycle costs.

It is relatively easy to specify a concrete item such as a car; it is more difficult, and perhaps even more important, to draw up a detailed specification for a service. Take for example the specification for a cleaning contract. Is each office to be cleaned twice a day or twice a week? Choices here will have more impact on the cost than anything the buyer can achieve subsequently in the course of the sourcing/negotiation/contracting process. Tactical and strategic decisions need to be made about the optimum balance between service quality and cost.

Another reason for buyers to get involved in the specification process is to ensure that the specification is kept as open as possible, and is not inappropriately skewed towards a particular supplier or item. End-users have a tendency to specify what they require in great detail, and not infrequently they base their description not on what they actually need, but on what a supplier known to them provides. Over-specification tends to limit the sourcing opportunities. Sometimes the users even provide a supplier name, part number and list price. It is then very difficult for the buyer to determine which features of the item are essential and which are incidental, and to judge whether a substitute (which might be significantly cheaper) would prove acceptable.

It is therefore crucial for the buyer to get involved in the specification process as early as possible. While this holds for both direct items (that is, raw materials and parts) and indirect items (operating supplies), it is even more crucial for direct items, as these will have an immediate impact on the company's end products. Once an item has been specified and built into an end product, it can be very challenging to try to replace it with a cheaper alternative that has a slightly different specification. This typically calls for technical support, and there are potentially significant costs of change. In contrast, if the cheaper alternative had been selected from the start, there might have been no additional costs involved.

The purchasing community draw a distinction between *functional* and *technical specifications*, and there are never-ending debates on the benefits of one over the other. In broad terms, a functional specification describes *what* the item is intended to do: the input, output and sometimes some parameters of the process. Technical specifications focus more on *how* a certain process works, identifying and specifying what is needed for it. Technical requirements are often given in great detail. Both types of specification have pros and cons. Clearly an advantage of a functional specification is that a number of solutions might be found to fit the functional requirements. The buyer has more options, which leads to better opportunities to leverage the buying position. The salesperson might have an opportunity to offer different, perhaps innovative solutions, rather than simply putting forward a standard product that fits the specification. The proposal might have better margins, or be something only the seller's company can offer. This gives the seller an excellent starting position for contract discussions. The disadvantage for the buyer is that it can be almost impossible to make an informed judgement when the sellers' proposals are very different. The choice often requires detailed input from the end-user. If the solution is an innovative one, it also becomes extremely difficult to draw up a contract and plan contract follow-up: the functional details might continue to be unclear until the final delivery. And it can be a disadvantage rather than an advantage for a salesperson to compete with a rival's product or service that had not previously been viewed as direct competition. (See the example below on air travel versus videoconferencing.)

In contrast, when the focus is on technical specifications, the very detail can limit sourcing opportunities. A salesperson offering a rival item can find it very difficult to break in to a new customer's market, because it is not possible to offer the exact known and specified solution, which is normally based on the existing supplier's specific offering.

A simplified example of a technical versus a functional specification

A typical technical specification:

- one airline ticket from London to Paris departing around 9.00 am.

A functional alternative of the above technical specification:

- a need for a discussion between people based in London and Paris;
- meeting to be planned for approximately 12.00 noon.

If the technical specification is used as the basis, the buyer will search for early flights from London to Paris with different carriers. The functional specification could lead to a much broader list of alternatives. The participants might meet in London instead of in Paris, or they could all travel and meet elsewhere. Those who travel might fly, or alternatively go by train or car. They might even not travel at all; perhaps a videoconference would fit the functional requirements at significantly lower cost.

Clearly the buyer has a much easier task working to the technical specification. Then the only issues are the timing and quality of the flights. But how do you value a physical meeting versus a videoconference? Do people want to travel, perhaps seeing occasional trips to Paris as a perk of the job, or dread the waste of time and the hassle? Would a train journey on which they can work be more cost-efficient than driving a car? There is a much better chance that the functional specification will, over time, lead to better decisions and lower costs, but there is more chance of getting it wrong, and more effort is needed to make the choice. A videoconference will not always be the right choice, any more than a flight will be. Perhaps for a meeting between long-standing colleagues it would make sense, but it would be the wrong choice for the first contact with a potential customer.

Salespeople sometimes see it as a disadvantage when a professional buyer is involved at an early stage in the specification process. They argue that it limits their opportunity to influence key stakeholders and end-users. It should be apparent from the discussion above, though, that there are also advantages from the seller perspective. This process opens up additional opportunities, as the early stages of the process are the best moments to make clear in real terms why your product is better than others. This can include helping the buyer and end-user to bring you in as an alternative source to an established supplier. (End-users regularly stick to the existing supplier as a default choice.) Even when you *are* the established supplier, ensuring a close cooperation with the buyer in an early stage in the process will avoid a situation where the buyer feels under pressure or 'locked in'. In these circumstances buyers can become very determined to find and fight for alternative solutions or sources. If you are not cooperative and upfront you might win a battle (the first order), but might lose the war (an ongoing relationship).

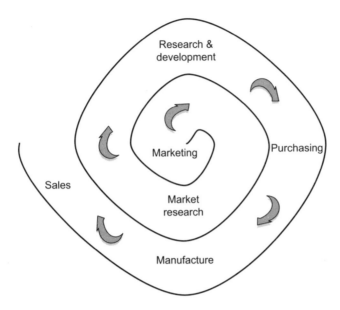

Figure 4.2 The influence snail

In *Key Account Management* (1999), Peter Cheverton described this process of influencing, understanding and interacting with other people in the customer organization as entering the snail (see Figure 4.2).

In the snail it is clear that purchasing does not have a full overview of all the requirements in the chain. Indeed it is true that any function in the chain can only see and understand its own part thoroughly, and understand some of the other demands to a degree. Each part of the snail has different experts with their own expertise. Understanding the entire chain is therefore impossible. It is always dangerous if non-experts try to pass on a message via another non-expert on a certain subject. For example when a buyer and a salesperson discuss R&D they are almost doomed to fail. (This is discussed more in Chapter 12 on relationships between buying and selling.)

If you focus on aligning yourself with the needs of the buyer, it is not very likely that you will understand the entire spectrum of purchasing company requirements, and key decision makers on the purchase might be completely invisible to you. For salespeople to enter the snail while ensuring a good relationship with the buyer they need to perform a balancing act, but they must do just that to ensure a good performance. A modern buyer will understand your need to have wider discussions and to talk to other people as well. However, this involves responsibilities and accountabilities on your side: buyers will react strongly to anything they consider to be unacceptable behaviour.

The next process is *sourcing*. This is the process in which, on the basis of the set specifications, purchasers search the market for suitable suppliers. At the same time they should be open to other solutions to the functional requirements, which could include changes to the original specifications. The sourcing process is therefore iterative with the specification process.

Sourcing could be done on the basis of new or existing specifications, and on new and/or existing sources, as well as a combination between specifications and sources. With new specifications, finding the solution and source is the key element of the activity. For existing items the solution might be more or less fixed, but the focus might be more on locating an alternative source to the current supplier. While finding alternative sources is an ongoing purchasing activity, in the last few years significant focus has been given to so-called '*low-cost sourcing*' initiatives, seeking opportunities in Latin America, Asia or Eastern Europe (see Chapter 11 on the purchasing agenda).

Sourcing is not just a functional purchasing process. In most cases end-users will have more interaction with the selected supplier and the selected solution after the implementation than the buyer does. So an interactive process of supplier selection and contracting between buyer and end-user is normally the best guarantee of success during the new contract implementation phase, and when running the relationship after implementation. Checking the specifications offered against those required and understanding the costs of doing business in the current scenario and in the future also require significant resources from both the buying function and the end-users (as well as from other supporting functions such as finance, the quality department and product management).

The sourcing process represents clear opportunities and threats for the selling side. When buyers are sourcing for new requirements, a number of potential suppliers are invited to support the process. As the sourcing process is very cross-functional it gives sales teams a significant opportunity to engage with people other than the buyers, making better contact within the snail. Given that the requirements are new, a wider range of solutions is still open for discussion. This provides the opportunity to offer a solution that is very specific to the selling organization, or one that gives a better margin (but not necessarily higher overall costs).

In an alternative sourcing process the sales opportunities depend on the organization's role at the start of the process. It is normally not desirable to be the existing supplier in an alternative sourcing process (unless you know that you *really* are the lowest-cost producer). Obviously the process depends on why the customer has decided to start searching for alternative sources. If this is being done because the relationship has been damaged, it will be hard to make an opportunity out of it. However, if the item has commoditized, it might be useful to engage sufficiently early in the process to safeguard other parts of the portfolio. You could even play a proactive role, for example by offshoring the item yourself.

Alternative sourcing might be also a wake-up call related to the life cycle of the selling organization's product portfolio. Unfortunately most companies first take a denial approach to such threats (like 'The quality is not the same', 'Our product is better', 'It will never work' or 'They are not really going to do it') and only take action once the customer has made the move. This reactivity is highly dangerous, as it is normally very difficult to reverse sourcing decisions once they have been made. Only significant price reductions can delay the loss of volume at the customer, and even then, buyers do not want to go back too frequently on decisions they have already taken.

The *negotiation* process is seen by most salespeople as the main interaction between purchasing and sales. Of course this is important, as it is at this point that specific details such as performance criteria, price and costs, and contract terms are agreed. While it may look like a predominantly commercial process, from a buyer's point of view there is a strong need to work closely with the end-user as a single team. The contract terms need to be aligned to the business requirements to ensure smooth contract execution. This is often not picked up by the sales side, and there could be opportunities to influence the outcome of the discussions by working closely with some of the other key stakeholders in the decision process. However, avoid 'working around the buyer': that old sales trick might rebound on you.

It is extremely important that the end-user and buyer talk the same language about the requirements. If there is any tension or disagreement between the buyer and the end-user, there may be opportunities for the salespeople to seek ways of resolving the problem. Similarly, on the sales side there also needs to be complete alignment on the messages from different people interacting with the customer, because different messages will devalue the sales offering. Experienced buyers and – more dangerously – experienced sourcing teams consisting of buyers and end-users, could try to take advantage of any differences in messages from individuals on the sales side.

The entire negotiation process is discussed in more detail in Chapter 9.

The importance of the *contracting* process is frequently underestimated. Contracting involves documenting the agreements made during the negotiation process, and this can be challenging in itself. It also refers to the process of 'selling' the contract internally and starting the implementation, which can require a major communication effort. It is in the interest of both the buyers and the sellers that this process is run smoothly and that the messages (internal and external, on both sides) are fully aligned. On extremely complicated contracts, buyers and sellers should consider jointly managing the communication by talking to each other's key stakeholders.

In today's litigious world the contracting process has an increasingly strong legal aspect. There may be complex issues regarding liabilities, warranties, different legislative requirements in different countries, risk management and so on. Consequently, after the agreement is made at commercial level between buyers and salespeople, a second discussion is frequently required between the lawyers from both companies to deal with the legal details. These further discussions could have significant commercial effects. People's understanding of the legal aspects of finalizing the contracts varies significantly, but experienced buyers will seek opportunities in this process.

For the maintenance of contracts or *contract follow-up*, it is important to ensure that proper feedback loops are built into the process so that on contract renewal, or on some other regular time basis, services, costs/prices, markets, performance and other aspects are reviewed and discussed with suppliers. The benefits work two ways. The reviews can give the buyer a good indication of where the issues are (if any), and where they can expect some internal challenges. It also gives them a basis to discuss improvement processes with the supplier. It gives the salespeople an early indication of how things are going, and whether anything is not working exactly as had been agreed. If the feedback is that the whole contract is running very smoothly, that normally means the end-users are likely to continue using the same supplier. It is never good to learn that there are problems, but if they are identified early, corrected fast and the lessons are incorporated into the next steps, this will limit any possible negative impact on the relationship. Most buyers would agree that suppliers that are capable of correcting mistakes quickly and efficiently are the most reliable and therefore preferred.

As buyers need to play a role in all of the processes described above, it might be interesting to understand how much time they typically spend on each. From my experience working with account teams, the view on the sales side is that buyers tend to spend most of their time on the contracting/negotiation aspects. However, when buyers are asked to list their activities, they give a breakdown more like this:

- market analysis: 15 per cent;
- strategy development: 10 per cent;
- sourcing (including the specification process): 50 per cent;
- contract negotiations: 10 per cent;
- contracting: 5 per cent;
- follow-up/vendor management/reporting: 10 per cent.

Sourcing is normally seen as the main activity, but as it is based on market analysis and strategy development, it is critical for salespeople to influence these activities too. If you support the buyers in market analysis, without giving it too heavy a 'smell' of sales pitch, you can influence their assessment of the market (but be warned, buyers are trained to assess markets from several sides, so blatant lies and exaggeration will probably not work). This will then have an effect on the strategy development and ultimately on the sourcing activities. If you have not taken advantage of opportunities in market analysis and strategy development, you can still look to support the sourcing activities, which might bring you opportunities or at a minimum could limit any damage.

Buyers tend to take the view that specifying, sourcing and closing the deal is the 'easy part' of the job, but aligning with internal stakeholders and spending time on 'selling' the deal eats up most of their time. A seller who understands this (preferred) time allocation might gain an opportunity to support the buyer and build stronger links not just to the buyers themselves, but to their customers in the chain.

The detailed purchasing process

Although this outline of the basic purchasing process provides some insight into the flow of activities, it does not segregate the activities into logical sub-processes, or define the links with other functions. It is critical for salespeople to understand the interactions with other functions, as these represent opportunities to influence sourcing and contract strategies.

In order to create further clarity on those aspects, the main process is often split into two core sub-activities: first, the strategic and tactical processes, and second, the operational processes (see Figure 4.3).

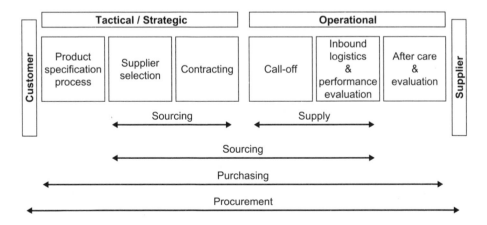

Figure 4.3 The detailed purchasing process
Source: adapted from van Weele (2000).

The *strategic and tactical processes* focus on developing the requirements for an item, finding (and/or developing) the right supply sources (including both in- and outsourcing) and the contracting process, which includes the contract negotiations, the legal processes and the (internal and external) contract implementation processes.

The *operational processes* focus on the execution of contracts. In other words they deal with when the item is required and in what quantities, and where and how the item is to be delivered, stored and managed. For direct items (materials or services that contribute directly to end products), this process is normally very closely linked to the buying company's enterprise resource planning (ERP) processes, and normally uses the bill of materials (BOM) and materials requirements planning (MRP) as a basis. In most companies the department managing these operational purchasing processes is called 'materials management', 'materials planning', 'inbound supply management' or something similar.

For indirect items, most companies have now set up processes in which end-users execute the transactional processes, supported by electronic tools. The strategic buyers set up a number of framework contracts, and end-users place specific orders under them, within their budget authorization.

The focus on delivery in the tactical and strategic processes is quite different from the focus in the operational processes. Whereas the focus in the tactical/ strategic phase is on definition of requirements, searching for the right vendor and ensuring the costs are right, the operational process focuses on the execution of the contract against the lowest costs. In other words, the aim is to find the optimal balance of costs within the framework of the agreement, including transactional costs (logistics, batch sizes and minimum order quantities), stock levels and associated working capital costs. These differences in focus require quite different skill sets in the people responsible. If a company is large enough to be able to split the strategic/tactical role from the operational elements, it will be able to optimize both processes by having experts in both specific areas. Generalists tend to be either more supply-chain focused or more commercially tactical and strategically oriented.

While this division is understandable from a skill set point of view, it frequently creates coordination challenges for the groups that operate the different tasks. The operational people tend to strive for 'no change' when things are running well from an execution point of view. The tactical/strategic function will always try to find new and alternative suppliers, and new and/or alternative products, and to move to lower costs at the tactical and strategic level. Buyers' evaluations do not always take full account of operational costs. They can argue for keeping the status quo on the basis that changes bring a certain level of risk, but if done to excess this will lead to paralysis and can even kill the organization. Each change comes with a certain level of risk, and even when changes are very well planned, a few (with luck, minor) hiccups can be expected as the two companies learn how to work together.

Sellers can take advantage of both these attitudes. An existing supplier can play up the feeling of risk to the people in the supply chain, while new challengers will find that it helps if they can show they have processes in place that limit the risk.

Another frequent risk is that sourcing changes are not picked up in full by the operational processes. Most salespeople have experienced situations where they 'win' a contract, but never see anything like the promised volume of business. Usually this is because the purchasing personnel lack the authority to make the change happen, or – more often – the communication between the different groups is poorly managed.

For the sales side this means that as well as having excellent contacts with the purchasing people, they will find it important to develop the same level of contacts with materials planning and materials management people, and with operational buyers who place specific orders under contracts. For major contracts and contract implementation, multiple contacts at different levels in different functions are crucial (see Chapter 12 on buying and selling relationships).

The value chain model

Although Figure 4.3 details the purchasing processes very well, it shows them in a silo, completely separate from the other processes in a company. From all the examples given in the previous chapters, it should be clear that in practice, purchasing processes require a significant level of cross-functional attention. As a consequence, it makes more sense to look at purchasing as part of the value chain, as described by Porter (1985).

This model places at its centre the flow of items, including after-sales follow-up. Purchasing is seen as a support activity, not only to the flow of direct items, but also to all other external spend items. This is one of the criticisms made of the model. It can be argued that for direct items, purchasing should be part of the primary process, just as marketing and sales activities are, as it directly influences the flow through a company. Certainly operational purchasing processes should be seen as part of the primary activities. Many buyers share the view that a significant part of the strategic/tactical purchasing processes, and certainly those focusing on direct items, should be considered as part of the primary process. As the focus on outsourcing major parts of operations, logistics and support has increased over the last few years, the management of this is frequently seen as part of the purchasing process, and by its very nature it should be part of the primary business activities.

Support activities

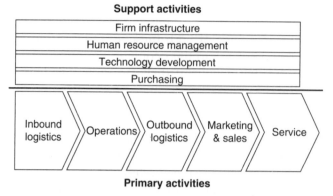

Primary activities

Figure 4.4 The value chain model
Source: Porter (1985).

Where purchasing involves indirect items (such as maintenance, repair and operating (MRO) supplies, travel, and office supplies) it might make more sense to classify it as a support process. So these two different aspects of purchasing, direct and indirect, have different characteristics and will fall in different parts of the organization. This has consequences for interaction with salespeople. For the direct items, more focus will be on how the interfacing works in the primary chain; for the indirect items, normally the link to finance is more predominant, so purely financial targets might prevail.

In terms of the development of purchasing organizations (see the next chapter), most companies start by bringing their direct materials/services under control before moving into the indirect spend areas. The purchasing 'control' in the indirect spend items is frequently significantly lower than in the direct spend, though the indirect spend could easily be 30–50 per cent of all the external spend. The wide spread of items is also a reason why purchasing knowledge is far less developed for indirect spend, and in-depth knowledge is certainly not available for all areas. As a consequence for the knowledge base, frequently the 'budget owner' is key in the decision-making process. This represents both an opportunity and a risk for sales organizations.

The seller's response...

The easy lesson comes first: know where the customer is in their process, recognize the different challenges of each stage, and aim to help them through, and do all of this while keeping an eye on the next stage, and preparing for it.

The more important lesson is: get in early. Sales people tend to focus on the negotiation, or rather, sales managers tend to focus their sales peoples' attentions on to the challenges of the negotiation – more training time is spent here than on perhaps any other part of the sales professional's skill set. Yet Jan Paul makes it clear that the more important task is to help the buyer get it right at the specification and sourcing stages. If the job is done well there, then the negotiation becomes so much easier (which is perhaps the most important lesson to learn about negotiation: preparation!).

Sourcing

The sourcing stage is portrayed as the time when suppliers will find it most easy to 'penetrate the decision-making snail' – it is too late to make the attempt (and dangerous, more to the point) once the negotiations have begun. This is incredibly good advice, but advice that is less likely to be proffered by the buyer in the heat of the process – so proceed with care.

One of the biggest challenges comes when the buyer is engaged in an 'alternative sourcing' process – challenging, that is, for the incumbent suppliers. The fact that they are engaged in such a process already implies some 'lack of action' on the suppliers' part – don't wait for this to happen; get in before the buyers have cause to start taking action.

Jan Paul suggests that the supplier in such a position – or better, one who reads the future well – should take note of the product life cycles of their offer. Suppliers get lazy, and long-term incumbents get particularly lazy. Products that were once state-of-the-art value propositions can become ordinary and plain expensive, and so the alternative sourcing process becomes attractive. Don't let things get to that point – you have choices.

One choice is to make sure that your products stay state-of-the-art. This is of course very easy to say, much harder to do, and potentially expensive, particularly if you operate in a market moving towards commoditization. Where this is possible however, it has to remain the best option.

Another way to ward off the 'alternative sourcing' bogey is to deliberately move the customer on to the kind of products that an ideal 'alternative supplier' might offer, and well before the buyer starts to think it a good idea to look elsewhere. Many suppliers have the capability to offer such products, but choose not to do so for fear of downgrading the relationship, or damaging their own margins. Weigh this against the risks of a full-blooded alternative sourcing campaign.

Specification

Before the sourcing task begins, the specification stage provides opportunities for the seller to work with the buyer in ways that many sales professionals still think unlikely – but that's down to their bad upbringing. Your first response to the section on specifications might have been a silent curse that buyers have at last got wise to our attempts to influence end-users with a specification that only we can match. Well, that rather serves us right if we used to do this behind the buyer's back. We are not forbidden from approaching end-users (unless we abuse our position) but we should be doing this *alongside* the buyer.

If you think such a combination will 'cramp your style', that may because you subscribe to the sales school of 'deception and low cunning'. Instead of trying to outwit the buyers, it is better to work with them to obtain a specification that will work, for the customer. If it turns out that you cannot meet such a specification, then you were never going to have been in the running, so you had best find that out sooner rather than later . . .

The many permutations of pros and cons to both seller and buyer of the technical versus the functional specification may seem complex (they are!), but it is within this 'space' that true competitive advantage is to be forged for the careful and politically savvy supplier. If specifying is not easy, then buyers will appreciate help from those suppliers that can demonstrate a genuine concern for the 'right outcome', even if it seems to point away from their offer. Involvement in this way can be of huge benefit to such a supplier however, raising early warning signs that might enable them to develop a more appropriate offer. Without such supplier involvement buyers may be tempted to take short cuts, which may lead to suboptimal outcomes for all parties. You must make your choice.

After the negotiation

The sale does not end with a successful negotiation. The good supplier must also aim to help the buyer 'make it happen'. So often the sale gets lost once the seller leaves the room. The supplier that takes time to help their customer build bridges between their own internal functions – particularly the divide that often appears between the strategic and operational parts of the purchasing process – is likely to see more of what was agreed across the negotiating table come true in the real world.

It is ironic that many suppliers to large multi-site, perhaps global customers, have such a capability, and often more so than the buyer. The irony is that this capability comes from their mode of operation before buyers started to centralize purchasing decisions – the local sales team. Too often, the silo-like structures within the selling company prevent them from putting the pieces back together, which is a great shame as there is a source of competitive advantage here for those who can.

5 Purchasing strategy

Influencing and understanding the purchasing strategy is probably the most difficult challenge for any salesperson, but it can provide an important opportunity to gain significant rewards. While salespeople tend to be good at influencing the demand for their items by working with the end-users, they do not seem to have mastered the art of influencing the buying strategy. This actually starts with understanding the customer's overall business strategy, as a good purchasing strategy is a subset of this.

You can map the customer's real strategy by reading official statements from their website and dissecting them, and by using the combined knowledge and information gathered through engagement with various functions in the customer organization, plus what has been learnt of the company's actual behaviour. There are some key questions to be asked. Is this customer:

- A cost leader? Then expect purchasing to have significant price and cost targets. Sourcing activities are a common approach, and commoditization of the purchase items will be the key strategy applied.
- An innovation leader? Then expect purchasing to have targets for new innovative items. Managing innovation becomes a key attribute.
- Geared for growth? Security of supply might be a theme for the buyers.
- Globalizing? Support in different parts of the world will be an issue.
- Diversifying or intensifying its business? This might mean major changes in the buying requirements. The implication is that the supplier needs to maintain an ongoing level of flexibility.

Depending on the answers to these questions, the purchasing strategy will start to emerge. A cost leader needs to apply different strategies in its sourcing than an innovation leader. This does not mean that the innovation leader will not look at costs, nor does it mean that the cost leader does not look at innovation, but it does mean that the emphasis will be different and the choices made will differ. The same is true for a global player that wants a consistent product to be delivered around the world, in contrast to a local player. Excellent regulatory support in multiple countries might be a key decision point for a global player, while a local player need only know that supplies are fit for use in the country in which it operates.

It should be evident from this that there is a clear and important link between the company strategy and the (real or planned) purchasing strategy. A purchasing strategy has several layers:

1. A general layer, detailing organization structure and set-up, including a people development strategy, and tool and process strategies.
2. A generic sourcing strategy, detailing how to execute sourcing processes, which could include strategies around e-procurement (including reverse auctions), or low-cost sourcing, for example.
3. Item-specific strategies, which are normally quite detailed and cross-functionally agreed as they require both purchasing and the end-users to jointly define what will be required, when and where.

In order to understand the purchasing strategy of a customer, salespeople should look at the following elements:

1. The organizational design of purchasing. This is discussed further in the next chapter. It will influence where decisions are made and what the execution model of the organization will be.
2. The sourcing strategy details. By listening to the buyers (at all levels of the organization), you can normally reconstruct a company's sourcing strategy relatively easily.
3. The materials strategy. Not infrequently salespeople and other people calling on the customer are a significant part of the input into the strategy. Being very aware of this, and making even more proactive offers of help, might create an excellent opportunity to influence the direction of the strategy.

A generic sourcing strategy will have a number of analyses of the current and future market situations, and will contain a number of the basic analysis methods and tools (which are covered in detail in Chapter 8). The key areas are:

- internal drivers, for example the importance of the materials, volume developments and key stakeholders;
- market drivers such as demand and supply, key suppliers, demographic and macroeconomic developments.

Based on the last two points, a sourcing strategy will be developed. This strategy will include areas such as the number of suppliers and type of sourcing activities (for example reverse auctioning, exclusivity discussions, tendering, core listing activities and supplier development).

The seller's response...

What tools can the seller use to analyse the customer's business strategy? The answer is, 'many and numerous', and so in this 'seller's response' we will look at those that are most easily used, that offer the best return on the supplier's investment of time and effort in using them, and that address the three most important business strategy issues for any supplier to understand about their customer:

- How does the customer aim to grow?
- How do they aim to win against their competitors?
- What drives them?

As well as analysing the strategy, the supplier must aim to have a positive impact on it. For each tool described below, we will also consider how a supplier might help their customer to implement their chosen business strategy.

Growth and risk

Figure 5.1, the Ansoff Matrix, shows four options open to any business wishing to grow:

- *Market penetration*: sell more of existing products into existing markets.
- *Market extension*: sell existing products into new markets.
- *New product development (NPD)*: sell new products into existing markets.
- *Diversification*: sell new products into new markets.

The percentage figure in each box indicates the likely level of success of each strategy, so revealing the importance of this particular piece of analysis: how much risk is the customer taking?

Risk increases as a business chooses more ambitious means of growth, leaving the home turf of *market penetration* and moving into the relative unknown of the other three choices.

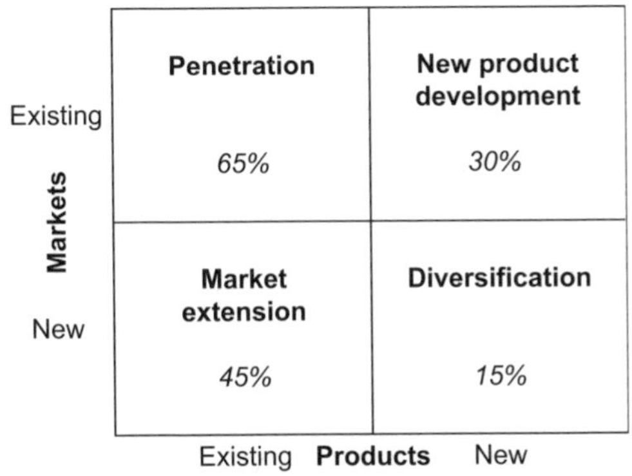

	Penetration	New product development
Existing	65%	30%
New	Market extension 45%	Diversification 15%

Existing **Products** New

Markets

Figure 5.1 The Ansoff Matrix

By reading the customer's growth strategy we also then read their risk profile, and the more we can be seen to reduce that risk profile the more we will be regarded as an important supplier: remove the risk entirely and we stand a good chance of being viewed as a strategic supplier.

The means by which we can reduce their risk will vary depending on the nature of their business and the nature of our supply, but most frequently will include: providing information (qualitative and quantitative) about new markets, speed of response (vital in the NPD box), technical and service innovation, providing expert staff, and training. Doing these things 'in partnership' with the customer, such as a joint market research survey, is likely to boost your importance yet further.

Growth and the product life cycle (PLC)

Figure 5.2 shows the typical expectations from a supplier, depending on where the customer's business, or product, stands on its PLC.

Knowing where the customer stands on its PLC makes clear what the nature of the seller's response should be if they wish to be viewed as a relevant and important supplier.

At the *introduction* stage, speed and keeping one's promises are perhaps the most vital requirements. Consider a food manufacturer launching a new product. Their retail customers may only give them two weeks in which to prove themselves. Imagine the catastrophe of one of the manufacturer's suppliers holding their launch up by just two days... What's two days, asks the supplier – and the answer is that it may make the difference between success and failure. At no other stage is 'on-time-in-full' so important.

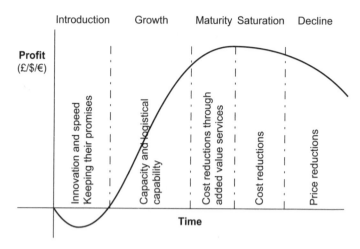

Figure 5.2 The customer's requirements through the PLC

At the *growth* stage, the issue for the customer may be dealing with unexpected success. Forecasting is one thing, but nobody wants to hold back a runaway success just because the prediction was for less. Suppliers that can keep pace will be smiled upon.

At *maturity*, the business turns its attention to reducing costs, and suppliers are perhaps the key target. The buyer may speak of reduced prices, because that is the easiest option, but as Jan Paul's comments have already indicated, buyers will be just as interested in other things that reduce their costs, through greater efficiency or effectiveness, and more so if those offerings are genuine and sustainable. Better still, a supplier that can help them stave off maturity, through innovation, is a supplier unlikely to be given a hard time on price.

If the customer is at *saturation* or *decline*, expect price reductions to be the main focus.

Their source of competitive advantage

With a good deal of simplification, there are two principal sources of competitive advantage:

- being the lowest-cost supplier;
- being a differentiated supplier.

Success is not necessarily the result of the choice itself – either strategy can work in a variety of circumstances – rather it is the result of the ability to focus the whole business on whichever route is chosen. For the supplier assessing their customer's strategy, the vital question is: can I help them with that focus?

Helping is not the same as matching. If the customer chooses to be the lowest-cost supplier in their market, that does not necessarily mean they will seek suppliers of a similar stamp. If your offer helps them to reduce their costs, let's say through operating efficiencies, then they will pay a premium for that and expect you to be, in effect, a differentiated supplier.

Equally, the customer that chooses the *differentiated supplier* route may feel that they 'apply the pixie dust' and seek suppliers who simply supply products at prices. This can be a problem if we limit our contacts with buyers. The vital task for the supplier in such cases is to be in contact with those in the customer responsible for the 'pixie dust'.

The customer's value drivers

What makes their business hum? What values distinguish it and drive it, and how do those values help their staff to decide what to do each day?

Treacy and Wiersema, in their book *The Discipline of Market Leader* (1995), identify three key business or 'value drivers'. All may be present in any successful business, but in really successful businesses, one or other of these drivers tends to stand out, distinguishing the business for their staff, their investors and their customers:

- operational excellence;
- product leadership;
- customer intimacy.

Operational excellence is about doing what you do well. It is about effective processes, smooth mechanics and the efficiency with which products or services are brought to market. Efficiencies of production, economies of scale, uniformity and conformance, accurate forecasting, slick distribution, fast response – these are the sort of things that might be important to a business seeking operational excellence. If this is the customer's lead driver, then the supplier must aim to make an impact on these issues – probably with a focus on the customer's supply chain.

Product leadership is about producing the best, leading-edge or market-dominant products. Businesses with high rates of innovation and patent application often have this value at their heart. New product development is very likely to be a key feature. Where this is the lead driver, suppliers need to focus on the customer's product, aiming to enhance it through creativity and innovation, and aiming to help speed any new products to market. Contacts between the R&D people in both supplier and customer may be an important part of this matching process.

Customer intimacy is the ability to identify with specific customer needs and match products and services accordingly. What distinguishs the customer-intimate business is their stated determination to develop close customer relationships and to act on the resultant knowledge at all levels of their operation. They will probably have a wide menu of products and services and the ability to mix and match these to suit individual customer requirements – or perhaps they will go further than this and offer a totally bespoke service. Where this is the lead driver, suppliers should aim to understand the customer's market, through to the end-users, and look for ways to help them enhance and distinguish their offer in that market.

Food supermarkets like to entice their customers through all sorts of stimuli, but a vital one is smell. The in-store bakery communicates messages of freshness, and the resultant 'good feeling' turns into a bigger shopping basket. The problem, for the supermarket, is that such facilities eat up valuable space, and are expensive in staff, equipment and energy. They are also very difficult to place in smaller stores.

A supplier of part-baked bread to one such supermarket understood these 'pros and cons' and worked to develop systems that would allow the customer to use smaller ovens, operated by less skilled staff, and so help the customer place in-store bakeries in a wider range of stores.

Their offer hit right at the heart of the supermarket's business strategy, as they wished to grow their business through a variety of 'smaller footprint' concepts, but wished to retain the brand strengths of the larger store format. In essence, the supplier was helping the retailer to develop both their growth and brand strategies, and it should be no surprise that price was not a significant issue in the relationship.

Whatever tools the seller uses, and these were just some suggestions, I hope the importance of this analytical task is clear. The seller has two reasons for conducting such analyses. The first is to ensure that their proposition is relevant to the business goals of the customer, and in so doing to help raise the status, importance and value of that proposition. The second reason is to actively help the buyer contribute to those same business goals, *and be seen to contribute*, so building the status, importance (and value!) of the buyer.

6 Purchasing organizations

'Know your customer' is a cliché in the sales field, but now that the purchasing function takes a central role in the buying decision process it is quite surprising to discover that many salespeople are not clear about how their customers' purchasing departments are structured. They have not fully mapped major organizational differences, such as how local, regional and global (central) purchasing functions work together, or how decision processes are structured and where control really lies. That lack of clarity will undoubtedly lead to misinterpretation of the customer's purchasing direction, and could lead to missed sales opportunities, as not all points of influence are fully explored. Having only limited understanding of the purchasing governance model can also create unpleasant surprises when trying to deal with a customer. Most salespeople can tell you stories about spending lots of time trying to get a deal agreed, then suddenly (from their perspective) finding that the decision was taken not by their contacts but by someone whose role they had not appreciated.

This chapter details the basic types of purchasing organization, and describes a simple model for making purchasing organizational development visible. Salespeople who use this model will gain a simple but clear indication of the main strategic purchasing themes. More importantly still, if and when the purchasing organization further evolves, they will be in a better position to anticipate the next level of purchasing themes. This will help them to prepare to meet the customer's future requirements.

One of the main elements of the purchasing strategy is the difference in focus between price, cost and value delivery. We also look here at the logical progression in this focus over time, and other changes in it.

Finally this chapter describes the different organizational set-ups, and the specific challenges they present, both internally and externally, regarding the 'ability to deliver'. 'Ability to deliver' means the execution of a contract against a commercial agreement. The actual delivery, in terms of both speed and overall depth, indicates how well the buying function (or the specific buyer) is established in the organization as a whole.

Salespeople who understand the purchasing direction, the purchasing focus and the 'ability to deliver' will find it significantly easier to manage the customer relationship and maximize the return on the account.

Purchasing organizational development

Driven by the functional developments described in the first chapters, most purchasing organizations have gone through a significant level of change in recent years. In summary the main changes are:

1. Moving from an administrative function to a strategic sourcing focus.
2. Moving buying activities from end-users to a team of professional buyers.
3. Moving purchasing management from a decentralized base to a more centralized set-up. This process has sometimes been dynamic, and some companies have moved to more central organizations and (partly) back again.
4. Linked to the above, moving buying activities from local buyers to regional or global lead buyers, followed by moving the agenda to global purchasing category management.
5. Moving from contracting teams to commodity teams, which are normally cross-functional.
6. Investing heavily in human capital by attracting and developing a professional staff of purchasing experts.
7. Moving the purchasing agenda in management team/board discussions from the cost of goods or items to a sourcing agenda that is considered a key aspect of the company's strategy.
8. Expanding the purchasing agenda towards a broader supply chain management approach.

As a consequence of points 7 and 8, purchasing leadership has moved upwards in the organization, and is now regularly operating at management team level or even at board level. The scope of a modern purchasing leader covers more than just the costs aspects of sourcing. It regularly includes playing a major role in margin management, change management, sales training, working capital management and so on.

All these changes have a significant impact on the salespeople visiting these upgraded buying organizations. While the operational role that procurement has played is still there, frequently as part of the supply chain organization, the wider strategic approach means that buyers ask different questions and look for discussions on broader issues as well as on price and delivery time.

Understanding the changes will help salespeople to address the buying organization's existing and future sets of requirements. As there is also some cyclicality associated with the move between local, regional and global, this requires a high level of flexibility on the selling side, as well as a good insight into the opportunities and threats that come with these changes.

With the development of purchasing as a function, the way that purchasing organizations operate has changed quite considerably. The spread and depth of the process has changed, and commercial agreements will reflect this broader scope, at least for the items that the buying company sees as crucial. The new generation of contracts or agreements for key purchases includes, as well as prices and conditions, specific requirements on service levels, innovation and productivity targets over the course of the contract. A simple price/delivery-date contract is becoming the exception for important items. Understanding this will help salespeople to better connect to buyers in the buying and selling processes.

It is important to understand that the same organization could adopt different organization models with varying levels of maturity for different items and portfolios. So the system could be quite advanced for certain items, mostly those that have a major effect on the overall bottom line or where innovation plays a major role, but the organization might consciously have decided to leave other categories at a 'lower' level of maturity. Actually that conscious decision to differentiate shows a very high overall level of process maturity. Often during this evolution the company decides to de-emphasize certain categories and move them down one or more levels, as the investment in them is not being adequately repaid. This is important for salespeople to understand, particularly if they start to sell other categories of goods or services to an existing client. Do not assume that what happens in the area you enter is similar to processes in the area you already supply in.

This organizational development is described very well in Van Weele's six-stage purchasing development model (van Weele, 2000) (see Figure 6.1). It describes the level of delivery, which increases exponentially with the development level, the geographical focus of the buying organization (local or central) and the purchasing management structure (decentralized or led from the centre).

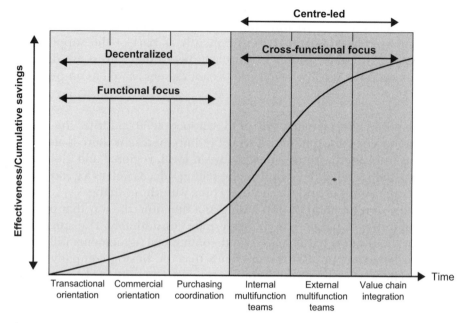

Figure 6.1 Van Weele's purchasing development model
Source: van Weele (2000).

The lowest level of purchasing development is the *transactional orientation*. Here purchasing is still very much an administrative function, where internal requisitions are transferred to external purchase orders. The function tends to be quite decentralized and the main focus is on running the administrative processes as efficiently as possible. Each unit of the organization has its own suppliers, its own items and its own processes. The purchasing processes are not seen as strategic, and sharing of purchasing data between units is not stimulated. Buyers (if any) are not key decision makers: end-users play the major role in the buying process. The key sales interface is therefore the end-user. However, it is wise to anticipate potential next steps in purchasing development, and build a relationship with any named buyers in the organization. This will provide an easier transition if and when the organization evolves.

The next stage in purchasing organizational development is the recognition that end-users are not the best-placed people to agree the details of a contract with suppliers. End-users tend to be too close to the subject matter, both technically and emotionally, to be able to scan the market objectively for alternative solutions. End-users come from all kind of backgrounds and disciplines, and frequently do not have the skills to oversee all the commercial and legal aspects that are part of a buying and selling transaction, the overall costs and the potential cross-references with other items or portfolios. So as the organization moves into the next stage, the purchasing function starts to work alongside end-users, becoming an essential part of the process, and starting to bring a level of *commercial orientation* into the process. From a sales point of view you can recognize this phase by the fact that the customer starts to ask for more information than just a price quote, and to ask for competitive proposals rather than sticking with an established supplier. The basis of a quotation is often a set of written specifications, instead of a conversation with or verbal briefing from an end-user. You'll see instructions for quotes to be sent to a purchasing department, often in a standard format. The buying company starts to send out general terms and conditions of purchase, and before contracts are awarded a round of negotiations will take place. The focus is still on individual units within the wider organization, where in general both the end-user and the buyer are located.

For salespeople, the change from the transactional phase to a commercial orientation is difficult to manage. Existing suppliers have predominantly had a relationship with the end-user, but now professional buyers start slowly but surely to become equally important in the decision-making process. It is not uncommon for there to be a significant battle for power between the purchasing function and the end-users during the transition. Sometimes this is very visible (and sometimes the end-user, or the buyer, will tell you about it) but more frequently it is below the surface. You run a risk of being caught in the middle of this battle. Any move you make might be seen as a loyalty issue. As this step normally involves purchasing taking power from the end-users, it is the end-users who tend to be the most sensitive to the changes. On the other hand buyers are often looking to win points or reduce budgets in order to justify their increased involvement. One way to achieve this is to change suppliers, which often happens during this phase. This is an opportunity for new suppliers, but a major risk for those that are already established with the company. Subtle manoeuvring is needed to avoid being caught in the crossfire.

Once the organization has moved to this first commercially oriented level, buyers start to realize that other units use the same suppliers, and often buy the same items from them. As the first lever to pull in purchasing is normally volume, buyers naturally seek opportunities to combine volumes to push for better commercial terms. This next phase in the development of the purchasing function is called *purchasing coordination*. As the units and the unit buyers do not necessarily have to give up too much of their independence, this progression tends to happen quite naturally in most cases. But in other cases power games make the going tricky, and it is common for buyers to bring in the end-users to assist them in a fight to stay independent.

In the first steps in a purchasing coordination process, the coordination is more focused on the volume leverage across buying units and on driving prices down than on moving the point of decision making. Sometimes people cynically remark that 'coordination' is a codeword for buying functions trying to show that they are making changes without having the guts to move to a real new set-up. It is crucial to understand that the decision makers are normally still at unit level, though several individual buying groups sometimes work together in different combinations to leverage volumes for different items.

The main challenge for the lead buyers is that if the organization is to reap the benefits of volume leverage, most units must move to the new negotiated contract. As the decision power is still at unit level, and units perceive that they have a veto, it can be a major task to get sufficient buy-in to new contract terms, a new supplier or (even harder) an alternative item. This internal process is mostly very inefficient and ineffective. Individual units might argue that although there is a benefit for the group as a whole, the move will actually disadvantage them. Buyers often need to undertake some quite subtle political manoeuvring to achieve the shift, and subtlety is not always a key strength of buyers. As a consequence, the lead buyers need to work constantly on the internal purchasing agenda to ensure that they can deliver on their external commitments.

For sales the challenges of the internal process represent a significant risk: if buy-in is not achieved, they will not see the contractually agreed volumes on which the negotiated price naturally depends. Often the contract volumes or the contract scope (in terms of units being part of the contract) are not reached, or are reached later than originally foreseen. There is also a hidden opportunity here: if the selling organization did not win the coordinated contract, it can still work to frustrate it and to keep business at unit level. This is not without risk, and is liable to generate hostile reactions from the buyers, but if you perceive that there are key elements that were not fully incorporated into the new umbrella deal, it can be worth working on the situation. You might find it possible to be 'heard' through local units that not only still buy from your organization but continue to send the message upwards that your offering is preferable to the main contract offering.

The level of internal debate in the buying organization often becomes quite visible, and buyers who feel – and tell their superiors – that there are still 'missed opportunities' (when units act in their own interests but deny benefits to the group as a whole) have a motive to press for the purchasing function to move to the next phase. The logical next step is a more structured and formal approach to buying activities. Slowly but surely, decision-making power and influence are taken away from individual buyers (and when they still retain any, end-users) and moved to the lead buyer. The main rationale for this move is that a loose coordination process tends to leave a significant gap between the opportunity (money on the table) and the actual delivery (money in the pocket) as a result of the inefficiencies of the internal process.

Purchasing as a function now starts to be more centrally focused (although this does not mean that it is fully centralized or that all buyers are co-located). The function starts to operate more with 'one voice', both internally and externally. Buyers' targets are set at group level, not at unit level, and portfolios are moved between different buyers and different units.

This organizational change normally generates a number of issues and problems during the transition phase. Unit buyers and/or unit managers often work to block the changes, but if the process of more structured buying management over the entire company is supported by general management, and it is apparent that the change is delivering real benefits to the organization (which is normally the case), the change will succeed.

For salespeople, this change too presents both risks and opportunities. One of the great opportunities is to grow business by benefiting from the larger total requirements and adding new units to the customer portfolio. Clearly where there are winners there are losers too. Small and local suppliers in particular often lose out in this type of rationalization.

An associated risk is that the chosen lead buyer might be more familiar with your competitors than with your own organization, particularly if that individual was formerly located in a unit that was not one of your customers. The best way forward is to work with the new buyer, while trying to retain a relationship with, and provide first-rate support to, the units you were already serving. It is to your advantage if they give your organization a continued good rating. This phase is predominantly about price leverage related to volume, as the buyer needs to make quick wins to show the benefit of the changed decision process. Be aware of the additional pricing pressure, and decide upfront what the new account size is worth for your business. This is not just an issue of margins: the key question is how important the customer is for the industry you operate in. You should expect the pricing leverage game to run for a few cycles, so seek opportunities to lower your internal costs in line with the price reductions so as to limit the impact on your overall margins.

While volume will always continue to play a role in the power balance between sellers and buyers (see the discussion on Porter on in Chapter 8 on purchasing analysis), at some stage during the purchasing coordination process the buyers will have achieved as much volume leverage as is available, or at least their efforts will be showing a lower rate of return. Prices will have been brought down by all purchasing approaches, and terms and conditions will be fully negotiated to the level that is beneficial for the buyers. Obviously small incremental steps continue to be possible (and will be made), but the big steps are over. The benefits of 'picking the low-hanging fruit' have been exhausted.

During this process, buyers start to see that although they have exhausted the possibilities in volume–price leverage, there are still significant opportunities in the wider purchasing agenda. These are mostly in the area of managing total costs (see the discussion on total costs of ownership in Chapter 8), which include costs of the entire inbound chain such as specifications, the cost of doing business and the supply chain agenda (smarter planning, optimized stocks, logistics and so on). Profit and loss (P&L) or balance sheet-related subjects like payment terms and stock management, focused on driving working capital benefits, will now get more focus. Purchasing will start to push to manage this wider agenda to continue to deliver benefits for the company. Their focus will move from *pricing* to *costs*. This is an absolute, fundamental and irreversible change, and once again it calls for a completely different approach from the sales team.

This is the phase in which the company sets up *internal multifunctional teams*, comprising a mix of buyers, technicians, supply chain people and finance people, to ensure that the buying team develops the internal knowledge required to move the commercial relationship with its suppliers to a costs debate. For buyers this requires a complete change in their working methods. In the previous phases they went from influencing end-users in their decisions to being the decision makers. This gave them a degree of power and stature in the organization. In this new phase some buyers could feel that they are having to give up part of that power, as others in the team will start to influence the buying decision quite directly. The buyer's work style has to change from single decision maker to facilitator. Needless to say, not all buyers can make this transition.

Salespeople can recognize the start of this phase when buyers suddenly start to ask questions that are cost related but on subjects outside the direct costs of the item. It is likely that functional experts other than the buyer will start to be invited to the discussions on both sides. Specific detailed break-out meetings are organized in functional areas (such as a functional meeting between the logistics departments of the buying company and the selling company), and suppliers are requested to join 'cost reduction' brainstorming sessions (in other words, value engineering the items). Buyers will still talk price and terms, but now they also start to talk about productivity.

If you are a salesperson whose customer is moving in this direction, you need to open up the debate on your own side, and judge whether your own company is able to – and wants to – match these developments. You (and your management) need to make a conscious decision whether it is worth your company following this route (assuming it is not already operating at this level), and whether it wants to do so for *this* customer. Moving into this new way of working together will undoubtedly move the discussion into opening up over total costs. It is important to decide *upfront* whether or not your company is prepared to have *this* debate with *this* customer. One reason is that fully entering into a cross-functional discussion with customers requires significant investment, and it cannot be done successfully with too many customers.

Whatever the decision, you can try to support the process on an 'as needed' basis, but at some point your company should take a conscious decision whether to make a fundamental relationship change (see also Chapter 12). This can be quite frustrating, because you can find yourself prevented from meeting your customer's proposals because the discussions and developments have not yet taken place in your own organization, or worse, they have taken place but the decision is not to proceed to a higher level with this customer. This can also bring into question internal policies involving the level of data to be shared with customers.

The questions to be asked are: Is this account worth that level of openness? Can it drive your business? Is there enough opportunity for the two companies to reduce costs in closer liaison, to satisfy the customer and your own company, at least protecting or even slightly growing your overall absolute margin? What are the risks of doing so and what are the risks of not doing so?

After companies have moved into the multifunctional team approach, there is a natural progression to the next phase. At some stage it becomes evident to both the supplier and the buyer that if they are to bring costs down to the lowest possible level and still make a return, the selling party must fully understand all the processes of the buying party and vice versa. Unless multifunctional teams on both sides have insight into each other's process steps and the associated costs, this position will not be reached. And if the two parties continue to operate as separate organizations with different interests, critical information will be held back (as you would expect in a more confrontational approach). So unless a critical next step is made, both parties are likely to see that the joint best position has not yet been reached. Either one or both parties continues to carry unnecessary costs as a result of inefficiencies or lack of coordination by the other party.

Therefore the boundaries between the two companies need to be broken down, and the next step is for the two companies to set up a joint *external multifunctional team*. This is a real key account management relationship (more detail in Chapter 12). The unified team seeks opportunities to improve results for both companies. In a perfect world this would mean that both see year-on-year lower costs and increased margins. Unfortunately the world is in reality less perfect, and the split of the benefits (costs reduction versus margin improvement) will still largely be determined by the power balance in the relationship. However, without any doubt, both sides should see at least some benefits.

Moving into a relationship involving joint multifunctional teams is a key decision that should be taken by the senior management of both companies, regardless of whether senior management was significantly involved in the previous phase. In the decision-making process the value opportunity with this customer or supplier needs to be weighted against possible value opportunities in putting the resources into relationships with other customers or suppliers. For a relationship that is based on external multifunctional teams to be successful, it is crucial that the companies' strategies, goals, targets and ways of working are well aligned. The real trust level, which involves more than a statement that there is mutual trust, is the key enabler or blocker of a successful process.

The decision needs to be supported and executed very well, and this could mean that different people are chosen to handle the account. A good sales manager is not by definition a good relationship manager, who has to operate more as a project manager than as a key interface (see Chapter 12 on buyer–seller interfaces and key account management).

There is a significant risk of failure, and this involves more than just the loss of sales volume if you should lose this customer. Close relationships between companies of this type are inevitably well known in their industries, and if the relationship fails there will be an effect on each company's reputation, which could extend across their entire sector.

Not many companies make a conscious decision to move to external multifunctional team working, and this could lead to major issues. A particular problem occurs if senior management are not fully aware of moves in this direction. If the salesperson steps into this relationship by inviting people from other functions of the organization to join in discussions with customers, and therefore gives the impression to the buyers that the selling company is engaging in this process, it could be quite destructive if at some stage senior management decides not to support it, and reverses the newly gained openness. Other problems concern the budget and timescale. Management need to be aware of the level of investment that is required, much of which is in employee time. It sometimes happens that managers become frustrated that after, say, six months there is no improvement in the profit from the relationship. The reason is simple: that is not long enough for the benefits to have worked through. The move to this phase normally takes at least a year, and while there might be some successes along the way (and the salesperson should try not only to ensure that there are some, but also to advertise them internally), the real benefits might only come a few years down the line. As with any investment, companies need to carry out an ongoing analysis of costs against returns. Of course, if after a reasonable time has passed, there is no improvement in returns to justify the investment, it could be necessary to cut the losses and move the relationship back to a good solid tactical/operational basis.

The final step in purchasing process development is *value chain integration*, in which selling and buying companies 'virtually' operate as one, and benefits flow between the two. R&D and development departments work hand in hand to create joint new developments, costing is jointly agreed and the selling company has full visibility over the entire buying company.

In this process the buyer and salesperson are actually only relationship managers, and the relationship has progressed significantly from its original commercial focus. Given the size and depth of the business between the two companies, major decisions are now moved up to board level in both. Most relationships will not reach this level of integration. The key drivers to even consider these types of relationships are significant joint development or investment, to a level that one of the parties may not be able to finance itself, and/or an alignment between complementary industries to break a new market open (and therefore almost run part of their business as a joint venture with another company).

This detailed description of the organizational steps in procurement development might suggest that all relationships will over time develop into value chain integration, as the benefits are greatest and therefore it must be a goal in itself to reach this level. That is not the case, because the investment increases, often sharply, at each of the intermediate steps. Therefore only a limited number of relationships between buyers and sellers will move to the value chain level, and then only for those items for which the return allows the additional investment. Whether this happens depends on a number of characteristics:

- the markets in which companies operate;
- the type of item;
- the strategic importance of the item (for both the selling and the buying company);
- the level of cross-company development required to design, develop and use an item;
- the opportunity (for both the selling and the buying company) for costs/ margin improvements on this item;
- the cultural alignment of the selling and buying companies;
- other major changes or projects being managed in the company.

A very mature organization is likely to have relationships at a range of different stages, as it has consciously decided how to manage different item portfolios.

In most organizations and for most items the relationships will probably develop to a position somewhere between a commercial orientation and internal multifunctional teams. Some markets do not have any relationships involving close external working, while others have a number of relationships at the last two levels of the model. The more custom-made the item is, the more development the item requires, the more an item is key to the customer's product, and the longer the potential life cycle, the more chance there is that the relationship will move towards the most sophisticated relationship approaches. Clearly there is not likely to be this degree of integration between buyers and sellers when they are dealing with generic commodities.

Price, costs or value focus

From the purchasing development model you might think that moving to the next step is a conscious decision based around the organizational set-up and organizational focus. However, it is more likely that the decision to move to the next stage is driven by the required outcome of the purchasing process, which could be any combination of price benefits, costs benefits or value.

While buyers move through the different process development stages, many continue to have a significant price focus. This might seem inconsistent with the model, which suggests that their focus will evolve as the organization progresses to higher levels, but the price focus never fully goes away. This is a consequence of the major effect the purchase price has on the P&L account (see Chapter 3). In addition, price benefits tend to be easier to measure than cost or value benefits, so they are frequently the key measure of buyers' effectiveness (and are often linked to their bonus arrangements).

Salespeople often question why buyers are not more costs-focused. One reason, of course, is that the salespeople themselves wish there was less emphasis on price, so they have more scope to negotiate on other aspects of the deal. A cost focus does indeed tend to give some relief from the direct pricing debate, but whatever their orientation, buyers will try to stay in touch with the market price and will not allow too large a gap to grow between market price and perceived cost or value benefits. And of course, in the overall cost equation, the purchase price normally plays a very significant part. Buyers do understand that focusing *only* on price may lead to them making the wrong choice, but don't expect them to say so.

The main issue involved in a move from a price to a costs focus concerns the expected time frame for delivery of benefits. With price negotiations, the time frame is short: the result is seen on the next purchase order, and the agreement requires only a discussion between buyer and seller. A costs focus normally means changing the way things are managed on both sides of the commercial chain. Cost engineering takes time. The first step is to identify all the cost drivers on both sides. Then it is necessary to understand how they work and ensure that the real costs are captured. In most companies this is a major issue, as hardly any company does full activity-based costing. Only when the activities and their costs implications are fully understood can experts from both companies start to work through them, trying to find a more cost-effective way of working. Clearly this requires some level of testing and agreeing to the new processes. This could involve pilot projects, and will often call for some investment. So although there are often real savings to be made, the lead time before they are realized is quite a lot longer than for a simple price change. On the plus side, the savings from cost-reduction initiatives tend to be sustainable, as real and lasting process improvements will have been made, while a price reduction only lasts till the next round of negotiations.

For the buyer the main question is therefore whether to go for short-term savings (which might be reversed with the next contract discussion), or longer-term, more sustainable savings. The two do not have to be mutually exclusive (at least in the eyes of the buyer), so the buyer sees them as waves of delivery: first, quick wins from negotiated price reductions, and second, long-term wins from cost reductions.

Any price-reduction, cost-reduction or value-creation process goes through a number of steps:

- pay less;
- make the item for less;
- find an alternative;
- eliminate a cost.

A move from a *price focus to a cost focus* is normally led by purchasing seeking opportunities for standardization, rationalization of specifications and a focus on waste reduction in the chain (both physical waste and process time waste). Purchasing will lead a cross-functional team to identify the opportunities and implement the new processes.

The next step is to move from a *cost focus* to *total life cycle costs*. Generally this involves the purchasing function project-managing cross-functional teams, internally and externally. It requires a purchasing strategy at category level, closely linked with the business strategies. Steps are based on clearly defined business cases. Specifications tend to move from operational to functional requirements, so the number of alternatives increases significantly. Purchasing starts to focus more on linking with R&D to ensure that newly developed items are designed to have the lowest possible life cycle costs.

The last step is moving from *costs* to *value*. The key issue now becomes the value that the item is delivering. For a buyer this could mean, for example, working out how to eliminate the item totally and still ensure the delivery of a solution with the existing, or a higher than existing, value. The salesperson needs significant insight into the buyers' end products, their values and where these values come from. Value analyses are normally product management/marketing driven, and the buyer is one of several individuals who provide input. Schematically this is shown in Figure 6.2.

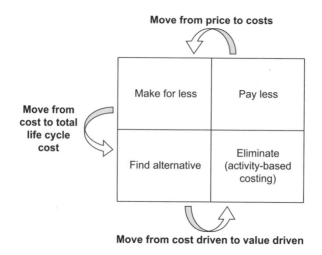

Figure 6.2 Procurement maturity: moving from price to value

For salespeople there is clearly a real challenge in the customer's ultimate value proposition: eliminating the need to buy an item. If you go back to your sales manager and report that you have supported the customer so much that they do not need to order from your company any more, you are liable to put your 'salesperson of the year' award in jeopardy. However, if you do not support the value agenda, you will put at risk not just one item, but the entire relationship.

Moving anticlockwise round Figure 6.2 increases economic value added (EVA), while moving clockwise delivers quick cash. EVA in simple terms is an estimate of true economic profit after deducting the opportunity cost of equity capital. It can be measured as net operating profit after taxes (NOPAT) less the money cost of capital. Therefore if costs are taken out of the system, it can have an effect on both the NOPAT and the cost of the capital required by the company.

Figure 6.3 analyses this reverse in direction.

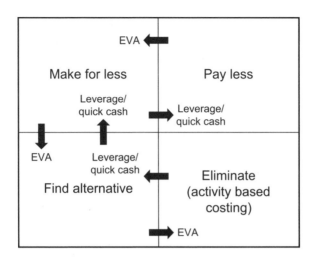

Figure 6.3 Procurement maturity movements: cash versus

The logic described on price–cost–value might suggest that the progression and steps are one-directional, but in some circumstances the direction of focus could be reversed. For example, take the merger of two food giants in the 1990s. Before the merger took place, both were on a value agenda with a number of their suppliers. The merger came as a complete surprise to most people. As the costs of the acquisition were quite substantial, the combined company needed to promise its shareholders that the synergy between the two partners would mean significant short-term savings. The first step in delivering the synergies was to rationalize the enlarged supplier base and to demand that all suppliers should reduce their invoice price by 15 per cent almost immediately. Hence the process moved from a value focus to a price focus almost overnight. Each quarter the company reported back to the shareholders the success of the synergy savings and purchasing was 'untouchable' in the company. That price focus remained for three to four years before the cost–value agenda was resumed, because suddenly the company realized that their competition was winning market share due to supplier lead innovation, something the suppliers stopped providing owing to the lack of profitability.

These considerations, and the progression in focus, are important to sales-people because if they recognize the movements through the different phases they have a chance to anticipate requirements and tailor their approaches accordingly.

Purchasing organizational set-up and ability to deliver

With the strong development of the buying function, the purchasing organization had to change quite significantly. For salespeople it is crucial to understand both the customer's current purchasing organization and its direction of change. This applies not just to the buying organization in isolation, but to how it fits into the organization as a whole. The key questions to ask are:

- Is the customer globalizing or regionalizing?
- Is purchasing moving up the hierarchy or not?
- In what mode is the customer working? Is it a cost mode (expect purchasing to be a strong and key decision maker) or a 'growth mode' (expect R&D and marketing to be stronger)?

Obviously it is sometimes hard to get good answers to these questions from direct information given by the buyer. For example, would a buyer really tell you that the trend in their company is for the purchasing function to lose decision-making power? Almost certainly not, but indirectly you might be able to pick up signals as you notice the buyer's requirements change. It is easiest to obtain valuable information from those who are less commercially astute, so it is crucial to use your multiple contacts in the customer's 'snail' and bring the information you glean together into one consistent analysis. You can often also extract a lot of information from a thorough analysis of the customer's public statements. In general this is an undervalued source of information.

Looking at purchasing organizations, there are many possible forms and set-ups, but they all tend to be variations on four basic models:

- local buying;
- lead buying (including commodity teams and sourcing teams, cross-functional or not);
- corporate purchasing (centralized or centre-led purchasing);
- a corporate purchasing service centre.

The first basic type is the *local buying model*. In Figure 6.4 the grey dots represent where purchasing decisions are taken. In a local buying organizational set-up, there is no sharing of data between the different units, and therefore the contact matrix for a customer operating this model is quite simple. Each unit will have its own buyers and end-users, who all need to be influenced separately by the sales team. The opportunities and issues you encounter in selling to one unit tend not to have any effect on your relationship with other units. Local buying can be just commercially based, but it can also be managed cross-functionally within the unit.

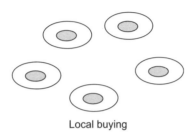

Local buying

Figure 6.4 Local buyer set-up

The main benefit for sales in working with a localized purchasing set-up is the lack of volume leverage, which gives you the ability to secure prices that are above the level you would need to give based on corporate-wide volumes. This is predominantly driven by the fact that the balance of power moves slightly in your direction (see the section on Porter's analysis in Chapter 8).

A second benefit is that in most cases the buyer has to handle a wide portfolio of items. As a consequence it is less likely that the buyers will fully understand the dynamics of the market, including the opportunities for sourcing a specific item, and so they might not be able to leverage fully the entire market/item details. Not understanding the market might also present a risk to the seller: buyers might try to negotiate over one item on the basis of market circumstances that are true for other items in their portfolio. The seller has problems to overcome when the same circumstances do not apply to the new item.

As a result, you can gain by supporting the buyer by providing market insight. This will help you to build a good relationship, while still managing to maintain better than average market margins. However, you should be conscious of the risk of setting different prices and conditions for different units, as over time the company might move to a more coordinated way of purchasing, creating difficulties for you. Buyers will not be pleased to learn that they had negotiated less good terms than their counterparts elsewhere in the organization. It is crucial to follow a logical pricing policy (for different units and/or different customers) if your goal is to keep a relationship with the organization over the long term.

In terms of sales efficiency, clearly there is a downside to calling on many different units, all with relatively small portfolios.

The buyer's ability to deliver on promises is relatively high in this model. When the buyer and the end-user are at the same location, the chance of the two being well aligned is significantly higher than when buyers and end-users are split over several locations. In addition, resolving problems between the buyer and end-user (or any other function related to this item) tends to be quite simple, as the end-user and the buyer ultimately fall under one management structure. Therefore a contract closed in this set-up will be pretty secure in terms of contract execution.

The relationship is summed up in Figure 6.5.

	Buyer	Seller
Leverage	Limited, own unit only	Relatively high as buyers' comparisons are limited
Pricing power	Limited	Relatively high
Market understanding	Limited, buyer has wide portfolio	Higher than the buyer, therefore good opportunities to 'precondition' buyers
Process efficiency	Limited, buyers have wide range of contacts	Limited, salespeople have to manage many contacts to maintain sales across the entire customer organization
Ability to deliver	High as end-user and buyer are close to each other (and could even have a hierarchical relation)	High as the end-user and buyer are linked, so the salesperson will understand the requirements well.

Figure 6.5 Local buyer attributes

The next organization model is *lead buying*. In this model one of the buyers takes the responsibility for the purchase activities for a certain group of items. This could be done in a loosely defined set-up or in a more structured approach (Figure 6.6). From the buyer's point of the view the main benefits are better volume leverage and increasing power in the balance between buyers and sellers. Because of the decoupling of the units (and their end-users) from the commercial decision point, ensuring alignment over the decision and delivery might be more difficult. Certainly when the lead-buying activities are defined loosely, implementation at unit level might be a real challenge.

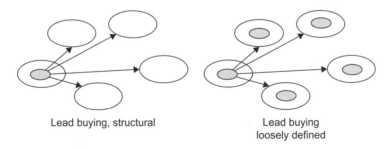

Lead buying, structural

Lead buying
loosely defined

Figure 6.6 Lead buying set-up

While lead buying has leverage benefits from the buyers' viewpoint, it can create some significant challenges. If the process of lead buying is not working very well, it is often because the decision power is not fully crystallized (so end-users feel they retain a veto right) or the lead buyer is not fully aware of all the requirements on all the sites. In these circumstances suppliers could find that after the original discussions and negotiations on the contract with the lead buyer, they need to carry out a second-tier negotiation at unit level to ensure contract implementation. This can lead to – or uncover – sizeable problems. A good example is a global contract that defines global prices and global volumes, where units subsequently take the global price and want to have the item delivered in smaller batches than had been anticipated. Other discussions could be about different pack sizes, different stock commitments or planning arrangements. Those could really add costs to your business. At the same time, in most cases it is almost impossible to go back to the (global) lead buyer to renegotiate the contract, as that would significantly damage your relationship. On the other hand, if you resist the units' unforeseen demands it will lead to more problems in your implementation process in terms of timing and/or volumes.

If a company moves to a lead-buying model, the sales activity needs to be boosted immediately. It is usually clear that the change will mean supplier rationalization, and as a consequence the value of the customer needs to be assessed on a different scale. This will almost certainly lead to price concessions, which require a balanced approach. If you reduce the previous price by too much, it might be interpreted as your having overcharged in the past, while if you offer too little, you could lose the business to a competitor. Existing large suppliers are in the most vulnerable position, as they are almost certain to lose out from the new arrangement, either losing volume of sales or keeping the volume but at a significantly lower margin.

When you have an established lead-buying relationship, it is crucial to continue to call on all the units. Too frequently (global) lead salespeople assume that they can handle the account by managing the relationship with the lead buyer. However, you will need relationships at all levels of the customer, including all units, to ensure long-term success.

	Buyer	Seller
Leverage	Increases as the volumes to play with are larger	Reduces as the buyer has potentially more levers to play with
Pricing power	Moving up due to the increased leverage	Reducing, as volume leverage moves more to the buyer
Market understanding	Increased, as the number of items/markets to understand reduces	Needs to increase to ensure the seller keeps up with the buyer
Process efficiency	Externally increases. Internally the ongoing discussions on selling the deal might eat up all the external benefits	In theory higher, but a significant level of secondary negotiations might be required to implement the central agreed deal
Ability to deliver	If the process is defined loosely, the ability to deliver is questionable; when it is more structured it increases. The buyer needs to be careful not to benefit their own unit over the others	Depends on the implementation of the lead-buyer process. If loosely defined it will be hard, but in a more structured process it will be relatively high

Figure 6.7 Lead buying process attributes

During the change from local buying to lead buying, and also after lead buying is well established, there is a significant risk that the buyer will be unable to deliver on all commitments. One of the key risks is that the buyer does not have a full insight into all the units' detailed requirements, and negotiates a contract that does not fulfil them all. A badly drawn-up contract might include a mix of the requirements from separate units, in such a way that the key requirements of a specific unit are not incorporated. For reasons of effectiveness and efficiency lead buyers tend to focus on the bigger units and expect the smaller units to follow, which is not always realistic. For the same reason lead buyers tend to manage implementation challenges more carefully with sizable units than with the smaller ones. Salespeople understandably tend to do this too, but it might reduce significantly their benefits from the coordinated contract.

It is therefore important for salespeople to agree upfront with the buyer how implementation is to be managed. Again, it helps to ensure that you have good contacts at all levels of the relationship. Before implementation starts, you could ask the lead buyer to support you in building contacts in all the units you did not have contacts in before. Joint communication, joint follow-up (buyer–seller) and joint contract/service reporting will smooth the implementation process and increase the ability to deliver. You might also consider linking pricing (and pricing concessions) to the success of the implementation.

Lead buying attributes are summed up in Figure 6.7.

Corporate purchasing organizations (Figure 6.8) are centre-led (though not necessarily centralized) and the function is run 'as one'.

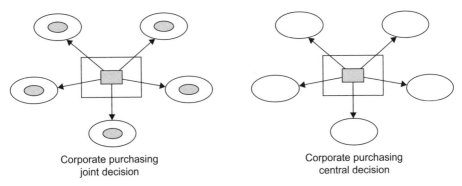

Corporate purchasing
joint decision

Corporate purchasing
central decision

Figure 6.8 Corporate purchasing set-up

It is crucial for salespeople to understand at a deep level whether or not the organization is really a centre-led organization. The decision power might still be at any level in the organization, despite the fact that the physical purchasing activity seems to have moved to the centre. A lot of companies claim to be centrally led, but buyers do not report into that centralized organization, and their objectives are set, and performance reviewed, by others outside the corporate purchasing organization.

If the reporting line between the buyers and the corporate organization is a functional one, it might be wise to carry out more analysis of the decision power. A functional reporting line could indeed mean that the organization is being managed as one, with clear result responsibilities at company-wide levels, or it might just focus on high-level functional development, some HR responsibilities (but frequently not even basics like the right to hire and fire), sharing of best practice and so on. If this is the kind of set-up, then it is crucial to understand the decision matrix and influence the key players next to the (global) buyer.

	Buyer	Seller
Leverage	Maximum leverage as the decision and the volume are controlled by one person	Most limited, but leverage due to long-term (strategic) elements increases.
Pricing power	High	Low
Market understanding	Highest as the corporate organization tends to invest in these elements more than any other organization	Needs to increase to ensure the seller keeps up with the buyer
Process efficiency	Varies significantly. Corporate organizations, particularly when they are physically removed from the units, tend to waste time	At first sight looks efficient as the key decision makers are all in one organization, but if they are decoupled from their own company's reality, additional efforts need to be exploited at unit level
Ability to deliver	If well established, high (though slow)	Slow but high

Figure 6.9 Corporate purchasing process attributes

Even when the corporate organization is well established and the decision power is well defined, a central model has its challenges. The focus and requirements of a corporate organization are also distinctively different from the needs of a local one. Generally more time is spent on strategy, market understanding and market reporting. This requires a different level of information exchange between buyer and seller. Also, corporate organizations tend to be less involved or have less operational knowledge of their own company; hence implementation processes might be more cumbersome, although this may not be recognized by the buyer. Dealing with a corporate purchasing organization means ensuring that the relationship at corporate level is well maintained, while at the same time the regional/local level is managed, as that is the level where execution is critical. Units have the tendency to oversimplify the market dynamics, while corporate organizations often overcomplicate them. Conversely, corporate organizations have the tendency to oversimplify the implementation challenges, while units have the tendency to stick to existing arrangements, as every change is also a risk. Units might feel that the corporate organization is slow and inefficient (which can be the case), as it always seems to analyse everything to the *n*th degree and to focus only on 'strategic benefits', while forgetting that there is 'no long-term without a short term'.

If the corporate team is well established, processes and policies are normally so well defined that there are no major problems in delivering against commitments, but it might take a long time before an agreement is met. Some of the challenges and solutions mentioned under the lead-buying process are also applicable to this set-up.

The attributes of the corporate purchasing process are summed up in Figure 6.9.

The last model is a *corporate purchasing service* (Figure 6.10). In this model purchasing is actually split off from the mainstream business, either as a service unit that is still part of the company, or as an independent company (internal or external).

The company might be instructed to buy only via the corporate purchasing service, or the units might be free to decide how to run their own buying, with one of the options being to use the corporate purchasing service. In most cases, as well as contracting, the corporate purchasing service is responsible for some level of organizational development, results monitoring, sharing best practice and general functional support, including HR processes. There is normally a wide range of service level agreements in place between the business and the corporate purchasing service provider. For salespeople it is vital to understand these detailed arrangements, and to take into account the relative decision powers of the purchasing centre and the business units. Is the purchasing service centre allowed to contract on behalf of other companies, is it a purchasing service consolidation centre for multiple customers, or is it just for the original business it emerged from?

This model is predominantly used for indirect items, where the service organization offers all units the opportunity to participate in volume-leveraged contracts.

The challenge for the salespeople dealing with these corporate service centres is that the take-up of contracts might be low. The fact that the purchasing organization is seen as a service centre, not a direct line management responsibility, might indicate limited cross-functional interface ability. The split of responsibility and accountability between corporate and local/unit/business-unit buying might lead to 'dual' purchasing organizations that could be in competition with each other.

The clear benefits of the model from a purchasing/internal customer point of view are that the service centre needs to be (internally) customer focused. The potential downside is that buyers do not feel in the position to rigorously challenge the requirements of their 'customer' (who pays for their existence). An organization like this will only pick up areas that 'deliver money for themselves', while many purchasing benefits come from 'attacking'

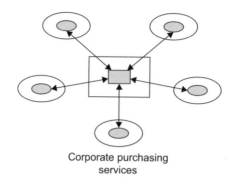

Corporate purchasing
services

Figure 6.10 Corporate purchasing service set-up

	Buyer	Seller
Leverage	Limited as they are a service provider, not the key decision maker	Increased, certainly if the contacts with the budget holder are well established
Pricing power	Medium	Medium
Market understanding	Might be well established, certainly if the service centre operates in a specific specialized field	Needs to increase to ensure the seller keeps up with the buyer
Process efficiency	Varies significantly, depending on the service-level agreements with the customers. As implementation might not be part of the agreement, the job might be seen as a project, not an ongoing responsibility	Could be quite personnel-heavy as the purchasing service centre has different requirements from the end-users
Ability to deliver	Ranging from medium to low	Ranging from medium to low

Figure 6.11 Corporate purchasing service attributes

the status quo that budget managers don't want to change. Avoiding this challenge could have significant costs/price effects, which could mean a potential benefit for the salesperson. And if the salesperson can influence the units or end-users before the service centre enters the loop, it might lead to better 'lock-in' opportunities.

If the service centre is run as a separate entity that is allowed to contract on behalf of customers other than the original internal customers, it could be handling a very attractive volume of business. Such a set-up is also likely to mean that its link to the original organization is significantly weaker.

The attributes of the corporate purchasing service are summed up in Figure 6.11.

For all models it is important to notice that there could be a significant gap between the direction of the company and the way purchasing is marketed to the outside world. Not infrequently purchasing is 'sold' by the buyers as a regional or global organization, with a central purchasing function clearly being the *key* decision maker. In reality, however, when you look at the overall business alignment you see a company that has split into separate business units with full P&L responsibility. Clearly this means that the buyer is un-likely to be the key decision maker. If you have this depth of understanding of any difference between the purchasing set-up and the company organiza-tional design, you will avoid major mistakes in the offering and contracting process. This will potentially create additional value if the sales force play the process right.

The seller's response...

This must be one of the most important chapters in the book, detailing the kind of relationship you can expect, and more importantly, *what you can expect it to do for you*, based on the nature of the purchasing organization. Jan Paul has given plenty of excellent advice for each type of set-up in the spectrum, so I have only one comment to add, which relates to your ability to take advantage of opportunities that appear as the purchasing organization takes on its 'higher' manifestations.

As the buyer's breadth of responsibilities grows, along with their power, so must the seller's. Jan Paul makes clear the potential benefits to a seller of working with a buyer that has broad responsibilities, particularly where they go beyond an individual site, business, or country, but these can only be realized if the seller has sufficient authority to act.

It has become something of a classic scenario where buyers have to deal with several different business units within the same supplier, and reasonably enough request a single point of contact to match their position, rather than having to see a separate salesperson from each of the units. Sound easy to resolve? It is remarkable the difficulties that such multi-business suppliers have in getting their act together as one, often because they fear the consequences of being seen as one unit, with all the ramifications of larger scale and discounts, and so they resist. Sometimes they may be right to do so (perhaps to protect their 'price'), but they must expect to pay another price for such intransigence, a price calculated in possible lost opportunities. Even if the supplier does not intend to resist, a sales professional with insufficient authority (or knowledge) will find it very difficult to work across the different business units.

The moral of the story goes like this: if you seek the most effective outcome between seller and buyer then the nature of the seller's organization, in terms of responsibilities and authority, and of skills and capbilities, must match the nature of the buyer's organization. This of course implies different approaches to different customers, unless they all magically exist at the same stage of organizational development. How far you decide to take this matching process will depend on how significant the customer is to your business and your future. In the realm of key accounts, this needs to become standard procedure.

One purchasing process where you perhaps do *not* wish to match the buyer is where they look to manage an item through the four stages of: 'pay less', 'make for less', 'find alternatives' and 'eliminate'. Helping the buyer to eliminate your product may bring a smile to their face, but is unlikely to do the same for your boss. The supplier wishes of course to hold the buyer back in this development – either to 'make for less', or 'find an alternative' – provided of course that the alternative of choice is another of their own products!

If the buyer has already arrived at the 'alternative' stage, then the suppliers must try to manage their own future. It will be of little use arguing for the existing package, the buyer's agenda has moved on. If you have alternative packages in your own portfolio, then this is the time to be offering them – perhaps managing a cost reduction programme through lower-price products, or by removing services from existing packages.

Much better; aim to keep the customer at the 'make for less' stage, through continual improvements to product effectiveness, or greater efficiencies for the customer's operations. Where this is the chosen approach, don't blow your strategy on one big and impactful improvement. Try to 'drip feed' the improvements over time. A series of 1 per cent improvements, lets say one each quarter over a period of two years, is far more likely to satisfy the customer, and hold the buyer at the 'make for less' stage, than one 10 per cent improvement right at the start that is then followed by nothing.

7 Buyers: types, motivations and rewards

While very useful tools and analyses have been developed for the professional buyer and salesperson, one of the main keys for success in the buying and selling process is an effective human interface. To adapt your style, process and approach of selling to the buyer, it is important to have an understanding of buyer types. For each different type, you should ask yourself what drives those buyers, what their key motivations are and what their reward structure is.

The next sections outline a grid of standard buyer types, explain their motivations and give some insight into generic reward systems for buyers. The combination of these issues will allow you to have a more focused approach towards any specific buyer.

Buyer profiles

It is not the intention of this chapter to describe the full set of characteristics of any buyer; they can vary almost infinitely. Instead we divide buyers into four different standard profiles. Inevitably these are simplifications of the reality, but they provide a framework for you to begin to classify and understand the individuals you encounter. These four standard profiles are called:

- the emotional buyer;
- the calculator;
- the convincer;
- the technician.

We distinguish between each type's way of operating by classifying them along two axes (see Figure 7.1). The first is their level of commercial content. This includes their understanding of the new purchasing tools and analyses, and the way that they implement these in their daily working life. The second is their level of strategic thinking. This is mainly focused on the link between their actions and the long-term cross-functional benefits for the company. Are their actions based on understanding the internal requirements? Do their actions focus not only on benefits now, but also on benefits in the future? Is their sourcing strategy linked to the strategy of the company they work for?

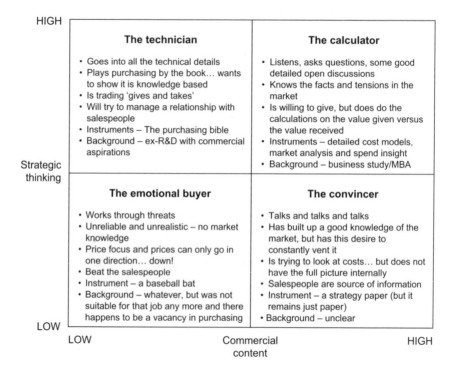

Figure 7.1 Buyer profiles

The first type is the *emotional buyer*. Emotional buyers tend to use power plays, even if an objective purchasing analysis would suggest a different approach. As a consequence they issue a lot of direct or indirect threats. These are based on their perception of the market, and can be quite unrealistic. Their logic is normally based on limited item understanding, and they are unlikely to have a deep understanding of the end-user's requirements. This type of buyer tends to stand apart from the company they work for. As a consequence their strategy (assuming they have one, other than beating up salespeople) is not linked to the company strategy, and is probably only focused on short-term negotiation/contracting tactics. As they are short-term focused and want to 'win' every discussion, these buyers are likely to be a little unreliable in two ways. First, because of their lack of true connection with the end-users, their contracts might not be implemented; and second, because they run with the emotions of the day, lacking direction from a defined strategy, they might switch between suppliers frequently, even within the time frame of existing contracts.

Their main negotiation tool could best be described as a baseball bat, their focus is very much price driven, and they expect price reductions every time they discuss new contracts. This buyer still operates without using all the available tools and analyses. At first sight you might think this is a nightmare type of buyer (in the eyes of the buying company), but depending on market forces and on the strategic importance of the items, they can do a good job for the buying company. If the market forces are in the favour of the buyers and the item has limited strategic impact on the buying company, this buyer can use leverage, hard-line and short-term tactics to deliver significant price benefits. For a number of items, confrontational tactics tend to deliver more than cooperative approaches focused on mutual benefits.

From a more strategic angle, this buyer lacks the level of thought required, and would almost certainly damage both the suppliers and the customer if they were to manage strategically important items (costs, developments, innovation or availability might all come under pressure).

Salespeople who have to work with this type of buyer should not expect to get a real 'value story' on their items. The discussions with this buyer will be hostile, and pressure will be applied constantly. All available tactics (fair or unfair) will be used to get the salespeople to deliver what the buyer wants. From where this type of buyer operates, it is a small step from normal behaviour to giving up all integrity in order to maximize the short-term delivery.

It is not unlikely that, because of their behaviour, this type of buyer's internal network is not very solid, and this makes them potentially vulnerable to end-users influencing purchasing decisions. While working with this type of buyer might be uncomfortable at times, the chance of their having a real effect in the longer term is limited (although in the short term they can hurt your business). You have only a limited opportunity to work to a wider costs agenda, and even if the agenda expands as a result of other developments in the customer organization, the reality behind it will be tested when and if new prices are discussed (at contract extension, for example). There is a high chance that this buyer will revert back to old and inherent behaviours.

The *calculator* is almost the opposite, and is a more silent type. Calculators listen very carefully and barely show any emotion. They might seem to share information based on a deep understanding of the overall business direction and strategy, but because they take a calculating approach, they will only share selective information. They are very capable of pushing back on sales information, but their push back tends to be to built on a better understanding of facts such as market conditions. Owing to their listening style, they will have a solid link into technical departments and financial departments – and very importantly, as their numbers are solid and they tend to deliver on them, they will be very well linked to general management. Over time the calculator will build up a good understanding of internal requirements, the market and the item-specific challenges.

As these individuals add up pros and cons, balancing all aspects on economic logic, they are willing to give in order to take, but they are in a constant calculation mode, judging everything in terms of winning or losing. They tend to use salespeople, and specifically the information they receive from different salespeople, to build a 'balanced' view of the market. The instruments they generally use are very factually correct: cost models and detailed financial analysis. Combined with the knowledge shared by the end-users, the calculator will develop a good, short strategy document, based on facts and actions and with solid numbers. They will see the final outcome of any commercial process as the result of the numbers and the strategy.

These people usually have a decent background in business studies, with almost certainly a major in technical issues or finance. They are excellent players for strategic or development items. They are less suited to operating in a combative market. And they might be not the best candidates for items with a lower impact on the bottom line, as they tend to take a lot of time to carry out analysis and make detailed cost models. They are not stars at quick decision making, so in almost no circumstances will they make final decisions in a meeting with salespeople.

Salespeople seem naturally to be able to work with this type of buyer. Most salespeople like to sell a story, and as this person listens and questions positively (instead of immediately starting to fight), a warm relationship is normally the consequence, driven by respect and trust and the buyer's delivery track record. The other key element is that difficult subjects can be raised and discussed, certainly if the rationale is genuine. However, do not misinterpret these people as soft buyers. All information shared with them is potential ammunition for further discussions and/or negotiations. The negotiation will be very fact based, very sharp on details, and their decision-making power (and willingness to stand up for a decision) will be very high. Fact-based and very professional salespeople tend to prefer this type of buyer. For some, specifically those who believe in opportunistic sales, this type of buyer will be difficult.

The next generic type is the *convincer*. Convincers are the type of buyers who like to hear themselves talk. They work on the basis that they have a good knowledge of the market, and are usually commercially very well trained. Their rationale is that they will get the best terms when salespeople see and understand their knowledge. They may explain that they look at total costs and that they are fully linked into the entire supply chain, but that might be less the case than it appears. These people focus predominantly on commercial trading and the market, and their internal network can be somewhat limited. As they have limited knowledge of the items themselves, while they can talk a good commercial story, the end-users tend to find they have little opportunity to indicate their demands and requirements to this type of buyer. In any case the convincer tries to push the price agenda over the total costs agenda.

Convincers often use salespeople as sources to improve their market 'knowledge', but sales professionals should be aware that these individuals can pass information from one supplier to another (as they want to show off their deep market understanding). Their instruments are well-articulated market reports. They might not understand internal requirements completely, as they see some of these as 'price-increasing elements'. As they particularly enjoy the process of contracting and dealing, these people tend to have a commercial background, but as they are not really all-rounders they may fail to link internal processes and information. As a consequence they tend to miss the company's wider strategic agenda.

Salespeople meeting this buyer will be a little frustrated with the interaction. They have a limited chance to tell their story; they will be used mostly to validate the buyer's 'knowledge'. However, if you share bits and pieces of information, it is very possible to influence these people's thinking. As a consequence, if you spend a lot of time with convincers it will help you to rebuild their story in a direction that suits your sales position better. In negotiation, these buyers will tell you why your price should go in a certain direction (and as they are not stupid they will underplay effects that drive inflation and overemphasize effects of deflation). Counter-arguments are either ignored completely or seem to have a limited effect. Hence preconditioning upfront is the key for a successful negotiation (see Chapter 9 for a discussion of preconditioning). Such buyers might have only a limited ability to deliver, as they lack the required links to the rest of his company. In addition surprises might occur, as they may be unaware of changing internal circumstances.

The last generic buyer type is the *technician*. These buyers focus mainly on the technical details of the items. As they are so focused on technical elements, they also take the purchasing process to be a technical one, and therefore they will play it according to the book. However by doing so they miss out on the capability to make the right strategic interpretations of the models and analyses. They will have invested the time to develop a technically correct model, but in their execution they will not maximize the conclusion of the analysis, as they will be more naturally focused on the technical challenges of the item. By demonstrating their technical knowledge they want to show that they understand the item background well, and they believe that by showing their insight they will always get the real story from the seller, and therefore a realistic price. Their trading principles are 'give and take', as these principles are closest to the laws of nature: action and reaction. They are relationship-oriented and will almost certainly have a good link to end-users as they speak the same language. They can build up a warm relationship with suppliers, especially the suppliers of items with great technical challenges. Their instruments are specifications and procurement user guidelines including formulae, tools and analyses. Their background tends to be technical. Technicians will almost certainly have a strategy for an item that is very much focused on the requirements of the end-user, but in their strategy the action orientation and the commercial tactics and actions will lack focus.

Managing technicians is on the one hand a challenge, because their commercial instinct might be somewhat limited, but on the other hand it provides a significant number of opportunities. The main opportunity is to build on the technical relationship with your company and move the item away from the 'commodity market' by adding technical features. You can improve the technical links by, for example, inviting the buyer to your facility, regularly showing them your technical capabilities, and assuring them that your company is a technical leader (only play this card if it is indeed among the front runners). If you support them with a constant stream of (pre-edited) market information, you will build a level of respect that the buyer will pay back in the form of loyalty.

Figure 7.1 shows how these four generic types map onto the axes of commercial content and strategic thinking.

There is no better or worse type of buyer. Using the right buyer for the right job is the key to success from the buyer's side. A misfit between the buyer's natural behaviour and the expected outcome could really damage the business (on both sides).

Of course, these are archetypes: you will not encounter a pure example of any of them in reality. All buyers will have a mixture of these tendencies, but each one's natural behaviour will be more aligned with one of the generic types than with the other three. If you use this model it will help you to assess buyer strengths and weaknesses and to find ways of working with them. Feedback in a number of key account management sessions has convinced me that salespeople find no difficulty in assigning buyers they have dealt with to one of these four archetypes.

Motivations and rewards for buyers

In order to deal effectively with buyers it is critical to know what motivates them. Here we focus less on what motivates people in general than on specific issues related to buyer motivation. The discussion of buyer archetypes made it clear that different types of buyers have different needs, but all of them respond to two key motivators, which salespeople need to understand and appreciate: their company's reward system, and the internal respect challenge.

The *reward system* will have an effect on the buyer's drive and direction. These days most buyers have base compensation plus a form of variable pay, normally an annual bonus system. On average these bonuses are lower than on the sales side – a typical level is between 5 and 20 per cent of basic pay – but the more modern buying groups sometimes rely very heavily on bonus-related schemes with much higher percentages available for success against tight targets.

It is important for salespeople to bear in mind not just the overall importance to the buyer of their bonus scheme, but also the mechanisms and thresholds that trigger different levels of bonus. Some variable pay schemes focus on the entire company's results. In that situation the buyer will have more targets linked to cross-functional benefits. In well-run companies the targets of buyers on cost management are aligned with those in other related functions such as product management, technical management and supply chain management.

In other schemes, the targets for purchasing are mainly related to price. This clearly puts additional pressure on the price element of the commercial relationship, even to the extent of putting at risk other important elements. Unfortunately this price focus is often found in companies where the relationship has a significantly wider foundation than just price. The rationale behind this is that success in price negotiations is relatively easy to measure, so it is well suited to form a measurable objective. Purchase prices also have a direct impact on profitability. Unfortunately, although price levels are extremely important, focusing on them alone could lead to a loss of focus on overall costs, the quality level, the level of innovation and other important elements of the purchase agreement.

More advanced schemes take a balanced scorecard approach, in which variable measures are used that aim to take account of, for example, overall costs as well as price.

If salespeople do not understand the reward system, they will fail to pick up, or will misinterpret, some buyer signals. If buyers perceive a negotiation stalling at a level that will cost them a bonus they might suddenly show additional tension, for example. If salespeople can find a way to agree a deal that meets the bonus requirements (in return for concessions elsewhere), they could avoid a level of aggravation. This is even more important if price increases are required (see Chapter 10).

While rewards are a key element of buyer motivation, a more hidden, but certainly at least as important, motivator for buyers is the *level of respect* they are shown in their own company. While purchasing as a professional role has gone through an enormous upgrade, a significant number of buyers still suffer from the feeling that they are underdogs. In order to compensate, for most buyers it is very important to ensure that under all circumstances their managers and peers take a positive view of the contribution the function makes to top- or bottom-line results. Salespeople should understand this internal challenge, and be very wary of taking any step that could undermine a buyer's position as that could provoke a very strong reaction. This is not just a risk, however: it also presents a major opportunity for the salesperson. For example, if you can give buyers access to information that will enable them to 'look good', that could increase their personal preference for you and your company.

Buyers do not like surprises. The key for them is to have suppliers that are always capable of supplying the items as requested and agreed. So your ability as a salesperson to ensure that the company delivers on your promises is extremely important. The buyer will have made internal commitments, based on these promises. If things go wrong in the buyer organization, the buyer gets the blame first, quickly followed by the supplier. Buyers also dislike surprises that are out of your control as a salesperson, such as major market changes, either up or down. These could undermine the buyer's perception of their position, so anything you can do to reduce the perceived risk will be appreciated.

The seller's response . . .

First read your buyer, then decide how to respond. The basic principle behind building rapport with people, whether buyers or sellers, or just about anybody in fact, is that we should seek to match the behaviours inherent within the personality type. It seems that people get on with people who look and sound like themselves. That's fine if all you seek is personal rapport – we could all learn to make our buyers like us.

The challenge for sellers goes beyond this however – they must seek to get the buyer to work in their favour. This will almost always require more than personal rapport; it also requires 'business rapport'. At this point the seller must assess whether the personalities involved (their own as well as the buyer's) will work to their benefit or their detriment. Jan Paul mentions the damage that can be caused by a buyer whose personal behaviours are at odds with their business objectives; in such a case all efforts must be made by the supplier to establish contacts around and beyond that individual.

Fortunately, purchasing organizations are getting more adept at placing the right personalities in the right jobs, so the issue becomes more positive: how to use personal rapport to further the business relationship.

One vital piece of advice is *make the buyer look good among their peers*. Perhaps the single most important thing a seller can do for a buyer is to get them promoted! This is not as unlikely a circumstance as it may sound – if the buyer does a good job because you keep them well informed, then their personal advancement will be, in part, down to you. For all their advances in knowledge and analysis, the provision of timely information to buyers by suppliers remains one of the strongest cards the seller has to play. It is surprising then that so few sellers capitalize on this. The fault is often that information is given lazily, dropped into conversations almost as an aside, whereas a more disciplined and formal flow might be more visible to the buyer, who will then be more likely to remember its source. Formal reports, particularly if they are prepared to a regular timetable, can be very helpful in this regard.

The news given doesn't always have to be good news. Above all else, buyers hate surprises – even nice ones can upset their plans! Aim to keep your buyers well informed, even if it is bad news that you bring. Indeed, if bringing bad news at an early stage means that you and the buyer are able to take action in advance of some impending crisis, then much will be forgiven for your role, if there is any, in that crisis. You might see this as a damage limitation strategy or as a means of working well with the buyer – the choice is yours.

Knowing the buyer's character and behaviour patterns will be very helpful in handling one of the most common dilemmas faced by sellers – should we bring good ideas to the table if there is a risk that the buyer will ask one of their lower-priced suppliers to take up the idea? You might say that this simply comes down to trust, but in such cases the nature of the buyer does also have an important bearing. If you are dealing with an 'emotional' buyer, your risk of being 'cheated' is higher. When you are working with a 'technical' buyer, the chances of them being straight with you are better. Likewise, favours done for technical buyers are more likely to be rewarded than favours done for emotional buyers, not because one buyer type is more 'honest' than another, but because their type influences what they believe can be achieved from a close and mutually loyal relationship.

8 Purchasing analysis

One aspect of the significant changes the purchasing function has undergone over the last 10–15 years is the development and implementation of new analysis tools. At one time the best that purchasing analysis could run to was simple spend maps. That phase is now behind us, though upgraded spend maps continue to be very important. Many of the analytical tools help buyers to understand their position relative to the market and the supplier base. They can then run scenarios on how to best execute sourcing strategies and tactics to maximize their own and their company's benefits. This kind of analysis often leads the buyer to create a cross-functional strategy plan for an item, an item category or a supplier. This material/category/supplier strategic plan will include detailed short-, medium- and long-term actions.

From my meetings with many salespeople, I have learned that most of them do not have insight into such key purchasing analysis tools. Most sales training does not seem to spend time on purchasing analysis. As a consequence, salespeople are surprised by the tactics and actions of buyers. They also admit that buyers have become smarter in the way that they play the markets and suppliers, and seem to have become better in managing the process to deliver the results they want. Salespeople also recognize that they have not kept up to date with the new analyses buyers use. They clearly feel this is a gap in their knowledge base, and they agree that not having been exposed to these analyses could undermine their negotiating position. If as a salesperson you know what preparatory work the buyers will have done, and what conclusions they might have drawn, you will have a much better sense of the scope for discussion and/or negotiation.

The next chapters explain the key tools of generic purchasing analysis. Not all tools and tactics are used by all purchasing professionals, and in some industries and companies specific tools are used in addition to, or instead of, those described in this book. But if you understand basic purchasing analysis, as outlined here, it will undoubtedly give you a better understanding of your own value delivery, and will enable you to start to working more effectively with the customer's buyers.

Pareto analysis/ABC analysis

We look first at Pareto analysis. This is not a tool specific to purchasing but is used by many functions, mainly to decide where to focus resources. It is a statistical technique in decision making, which is used for selecting a limited number of tasks that produce a significant overall effect. It uses the Pareto principle (also known as the 80–20 rule), which states that for many phenomena, 80 per cent of the consequences stem from 20 per cent of the causes. The idea here is that by doing 20 per cent of the work you can generate 80 per cent of the advantage available. This is a common rule of thumb in business: it is often claimed, for instance, that '80 per cent of your sales come from 20 per cent of your clients' or that in terms of purchasing results (that is, savings), a large majority of the result (80 per cent) could be captured by focusing on a small part of the purchasing portfolio (the top 20 per cent of spend).

A Pareto curve is shown in Figure 8.1.

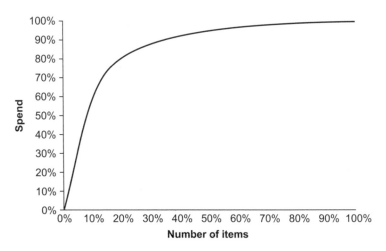

Figure 8.1 Pareto analysis

A purchasing Pareto analysis is very basic, but it is useful for buyers when purchasing starts to get increased attention and when there is relatively little purchasing history. It helps to focus on the 'big ticket' items, or to use another metaphor, to pick 'the low-hanging fruit'. In this way the purchasing department can create momentum by showing a delivery track record, and this creates support that will ensure ongoing creation of benefits.

A Pareto analysis continues to be useful during or in preparation for major changes, like mergers or acquisitions, technological changes, shortages and allocations. In managing these changes and challenges, it normally works very well to focus first on the key items, and then – only after these changes have been successfully implemented – to execute the changes in the tail end of the portfolio.

However Pareto analysis has a number of intrinsic risks:

- It restricts the search for opportunities to a limited number of items. While this is efficient to start with, at some stage the easy opportunities tend to have already been captured. The next 10 per cent of spend (with a significant higher number of items) could then be an excellent source for delivering the next set of benefits.
- The 20 per cent is often defined as spend. However, while spend is important for a company, the sales level associated with an item might be more important. For example, instead of looking at the top 20 per cent of items by purchase value, you could ask which 20 per cent of the items are the most critical to achieving company results.
- If spends of specific items fluctuate significantly, items could drift in and out of the 20 per cent zone. These types of item require significant attention as they will have significant bottom-line effects.
- Continuing to look at the top items does not drive improvements coming from simplification and standardization or harmonization. Overall supply chain savings from reducing the tail end could be significantly larger than those found just by looking at price savings in the top 20 per cent spend (and continue after those have been largely captured).

An example of the risk mentioned in the second point (looking at the impact of an item instead of purchasing spend) comes from a speciality chemical company. The company has a turnover of about $1 million and a purchasing spend on direct items of about $0.5 million, across almost 6,000 items. It had done an excellent Pareto analysis and made sure it was followed through to focus on the items that made up 20 per cent of the spend. There were just 400 of these, and the purchasing team worked very hard to ensure that they secured supply for these top 400 spend items. However, when the purchasing spend was linked through to the bill for materials, and the associated sales values were linked to the items, in the Pareto of the most important raw materials for the company's turnover it was suddenly found the second most important item was one that involved a very limited spend. In the original Pareto analysis of purchasing spend, it could only be found around the 2,000th place in terms of importance. A short time later there was a shortage of this material on world markets, and it became even clearer that focusing strategies and tactics only on the items that made up 20 per cent of the spend was not aligned with the overall benefits and risks for the company.

An example of an issue relating to the third point in the list (sharply fluctuating item prices) comes from a food company. It too had done a Pareto analysis, and one particular agricultural product was not among the key 20 per cent of the items. At the time of the analysis the product was trading at $12 per kg. The following year, however, the product was one of the largest spend items, as the price had increased to over $500 per kg. Two years later the price was below $20 per kg again. Managing both availability and pricing in the rally up and in the 'free fall' down required quite a robust process. As the original Pareto analysis did not list this product, the rally up hit the company quite hard – probably harder than would have happened if the Pareto had been adjusted for rapid pricing changes.

A similar analysis to the Pareto analysis is the ABC classification (Figure 8.2). This divides all the purchased items into three categories. The classification is mostly made on the basis of purchasing spend by item or by item category, but could equally be on the basis of importance to the buying company. The division between A, B and C items is made on the basis of:

- **A** – A small group of items representing a major part of the total spend. The greatest consideration is given to this category.
- **B** – An intermediate collection of items that is given less consideration.
- **C** – A large collection of items representing only a minor part of the total spend. In contrast, this category is given the least consideration.

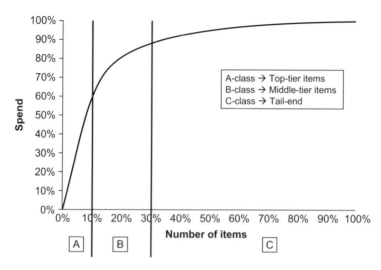

Figure 8.2 ABC analysis

Now let's consider the relevance of Pareto analysis and the ABC classification for salespeople. Clearly you will find it useful to understand where the items you have to sell sit in the classification, because this will give you a clue to how the buyer will behave. If your product is something that will clearly rate in the top 20 per cent (or the A group) for this customer, it means significant attention will be given to the purchase. You can expect buyers to develop detailed purchasing strategies, as well as actions to maximize short-term delivery. The focus on savings will recur each time the company goes through major changes that focus on cash delivery.

If your product is likely to rate in the B category, or even the C category (or is out of the target zone of a Pareto analysis), this will mean that you are subject to less immediate short-term pressure from the buyer. On the other hand, the fact that you receive less attention from the buyer will make it more difficult to develop the relationship further (and therefore grow the sales portfolio).

On C items, you will start to see a risk of tailored products being rationalized or harmonized out in favour of cheaper generics. If an item is clearly in the tail of the customer's portfolio, one question that should be asked is where it features in your own company's portfolio. Does this item make an average-to-good return, or is it something provided as a service, an item the customer has asked you to provide to complete your offering to them? Are your internal costings thorough enough to enable you to judge whether you could live with withdrawal of this item? (A harsh look at costs might even show that when overheads are correctly allocated, the company makes a loss in providing such marginal items.) Would it be perhaps a good idea if you took the lead in suggesting a review of the customer's need for the item? You would then be seen to 'support' the customer in starting a rationalization/harmonization process, which would enable them to cut the tail and make savings.

Kraljic analysis

The Kraljic analysis (named after Dr Peter Kraljic from McKinsey) is one of the most important of all purchasing analyses. It links the importance and risk of an item to an appropriate sourcing strategy. So if you understand how your buyer uses this tool, you have a chance to anticipate the buyer's sourcing strategies and put the buying actions into perspective.

A number of very useful variants have been developed by several leading experts in purchasing, with minor differences in focus and some variation in naming the axes, which are all based on the standard two-by-two Boston matrix. As all of these variants are very similar, we shall focus on just two, the original Kraljic matrix and the Van Weele purchasing portfolio model.

The Kraljic matrix tries to plot supply risk against the impact on financial results by spend category. Neither axis is defined in much detail, and this leaves a lot open to interpretation. (However, the model is meant to generate insights, not to serve as a numerically accurate graph.) For this reason there is not necessarily a scale on the axes, but the items are plotted relative to each other.

Supply risks should be seen as the difficulty of getting sufficient suppliers to ensure a secure supply of any specific item. Another way of looking at this is to ask how 'special' the item is. In general items with a high number of suppliers, and items that are sourced 'off the shelf' or are easily exchangeable with other items, have a low supply risk. In contrast, items that are customized or fully custom designed and/or patented have a significantly higher supply risk. However, it is a little more complicated than this, as even relatively standard products could have supply risks associated with them. Good examples are crop-related products. In nine years out of 10 there could be sufficient suppliers and volumes available, but a bad harvest could create a sudden shortage. And if a standard item is bought in much greater volumes by one customer than by others, the item will pose a higher supply risk for the large buyer, which would be much more vulnerable to changes in supply and demand. Although there may be plenty of suppliers offering the item, this does not mean that the risks are small for this large buyer. However, smaller buyers of the same item would probably classify it as 'low supply risk'. Last but not least, the supply risk needs to be reviewed holistically, including risks farther back in the chain. For example, many suppliers could perhaps supply the component that you require, but they might all use the same base raw material, and that might be in short supply. The fact that the buyer has multiple sources, all with sufficient capacity and capability, does not take away a supply risk earlier in the chain, which needs to be considered in the supply risk analysis.

Impact on financial results is in principle a measurable parameter: you can calculate the effect of an item on the company's financial results, although the Boston matrix only requires a high/low classification, and so it is usual to simply judge items relative to each other. One way of doing the calculation is by estimating the sales that would be lost if the item were not available. Other variants of looking at the impact on the financial results are also used, but tend to lead to a similar answer. Some companies that find problems in carrying out this analysis use the purchase value on this axis. However that could easily disturb the results (see the comments above on a similar challenge in Pareto or ABC analysis).

Items with relatively high supply risks are placed on the right of the matrix, and those with the highest impact on the bottom line at the top. The four boxes then indicate the appropriate basic purchasing sourcing strategy (see Figure 8.3).

Figure 8.3 Kraljic matrix with procurement management focus

If the supply risk is low and the impact on the financial results is also low, it is clear that the resources devoted to purchasing should be limited too. There needs to be a lot of focus on efficient transactions, and this is called *purchasing management*. As the costs of items will not have a major influence on the results of the company, sourcing and negotiation efforts need to be limited to annual or biannual one-off events, followed up by a simple transaction process when goods are ordered under the agreement.

If the supply risk is low (because there are plenty of supplies and suppliers, and therefore significant competition), but there is a significant effect on the buying company's bottom line, the main focus will be on price negotiation. This category is called *materials management*.

If the supply risk is significantly higher, but the effect on the financial results is still limited, getting the materials or services is key, and the cost is much less of a factor. Sourcing is the key to the success here, so this box is called *sourcing management*.

Finally we have the area where both the supply risk and the effect on the bottom line are high. This is where the buyer needs to put effort into ensuring a reliable supply at a competitive cost, so this box is called *supply management*. This is the area where the buyer will try to seek a stronger relationship with the seller, focusing on total costs and working together over the long term.

Summarizing the different areas in terms of focus, key performance criteria, sources of supply, time horizons, items falling in each category and the purchasing decision process, Kraljic developed the matrix shown as Figure 8.4.

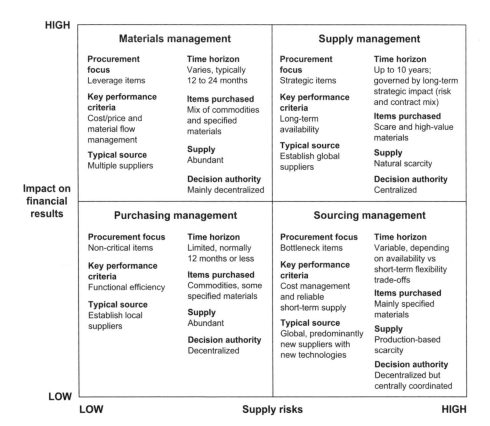

Figure 8.4 Kraljic matrix with procurement management attributes

This model was developed further by several people. One of the most useful additions was made by Professor Arjan van Weele, who linked the different sourcing and purchasing categories with the associated sourcing strategy. He gave the four boxes slightly different names, but the base principles remained the same. This is extremely useful for buyers in moving from the analysis into a sourcing strategy. Figure 8.5 shows Van Weele's model.

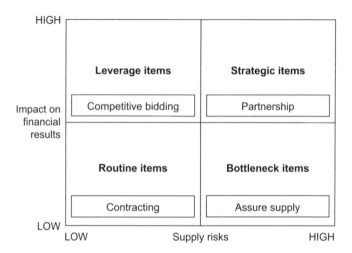

Figure 8.5 Kraljic matrix with sourcing strategies, adapted by van Weele

Items with a high supply risk and high impact on the bottom line are called *strategic items*. The basic sourcing strategy here is to build solid relationships with the key suppliers to ensure sustainable competitive advantage. This is sometimes referred to as 'partnership', although that word is regularly misused by both buyers and sellers.

Items with a high supply risk but limited effect on the bottom line are referred to as *bottleneck items*. The basic sourcing strategy here is to ensure a reliable supply. This could be achieved by building a stronger relationship with the supplier (not necessarily a partnership, as spend on this item might be relatively low), as a high focus on the vendor relationship is required to ensure short-term supplies. At the same time, a major 'alternative sourcing' process (alternative materials/services or suppliers) might be triggered in the buying company if it believes that obtaining item will be more problematic in the future.

Items with a high impact on the financial results but limited supply risks are called *leverage items*. It could be argued that this box represents a 'buyer's paradise': many suppliers with the same or similar offerings, and a spend that is high enough to have an effect on the corporate bottom line. The base sourcing strategy is competitive bidding based on a relatively strong buying position (since there are a lot of competing vendors). All kind of tools that force leverage will be used by the buyer, including requests for quotation (RFQs), reverse auctions, hardball playing by the buyer, price focus and one-off focus. This is typically the area in which buyers seek opportunities through using modern e-tools like (reverse) auctions on the internet (see the section on e-sourcing in Chapter 11 on this).

The last category is of items with low impact on the bottom line and low supply risk, which are called *routine items*. The basic strategy for dealing with these items is contracting, and effective and efficient management of the transactions. E-catalogues are among the solutions frequently used for these types of material or service.

It is important to plot items on the matrix and review their relative positions, and therefore the appropriate sourcing strategy, on a regular basis, as the item positions are not static. Changes can be driven by alterations in the supply situation (market drivers, life cycle of items, service offering, active suppliers, costing of materials) and/or the impact on the company (due to demand movements or alternatives or innovations), and items can move significantly in their matrix positioning.

A newly introduced item could be, for example, either a replacement for an existing one that had a significant overall purchase cost, so that it immediately has a significant effect on financial results, or it might be linked to a new end product, where the purchase volume will initially at least be low. A replacement item will normally enter the matrix in the strategic area or the leverage area, while one required for an innovation tends to enter the matrix in the bottleneck area.

A bottleneck item can develop in any of three ways:

- It could remain a bottleneck item forever, until it reaches the end of the life cycle. The item is required by the buying company, but the overall impact on its bottom line remains limited.
- Increased internal need for the item – perhaps because a product in which it is incorporated grows in sales volume – will mean that it has increased impact on the bottom line. The item will move to the strategic category, if sourcing remains limited. Alternatively, the success may mean that many other suppliers start offering this item, the supply risk reduces significantly and it moves to the leverage category.
- The product could become a success, but unfortunately the item still continues to be difficult to obtain, or otherwise subject to supply risk. Perhaps a sole supplier has it protected with patents, or there are specific characteristics that other suppliers seem unable to replicate. It is also possible that the buyer will fail to convince product management and/or the technical community that the risk is sufficient to justify putting effort

into establishing alternative supply sources. The item then becomes a strategic item.

Strategic items could move to the leverage category if the buyer is successful in 'commoditizing' the business by increasing supply opportunities. This could be done through focused (low-cost) sourcing initiatives. In contrast, leverage items could become more restricted in their availability over time. This only tends to happen at the end of the life cycle for an item. As overall market demand declines, the number of suppliers will also fall, but perhaps a specific customer might continue to have a need for the item. The risk of supply goes up, so a leverage item could become a more strategic item. Then over time, when this last customer too finds that the market is disappearing, the item has less effect on the bottom line and it could end up in the bottleneck category.

Another possibility for items in the leverage category is that at the end of the life cycle of the products that use them, plenty of producers continue to offer those items. So there will be limited supply risk, but the effect on the bottom line gets smaller and the item might move to the routine category.

In a limited number of cases, and for niche usage, it is even possible that items once in the routine category will become bottleneck items as many producers decide to quit the market, causing the supply risk to increase so much that the item moves to the right.

From a buyer's point of view, moving supply risk downwards increases the level of direct pricing benefits, because there is an increased chance of competitive sourcing. Commoditizing items increases buyers' potential leverage. Good buyers will always argue internally that when a new product generates a requirement for a new supply item, there must be at least two potential sources to avoid high supply risks. The risk to the buying company increases even further when products that incorporate items with a high supply risk are more successful, adding to the effect on the bottom line. From a functional buying point of view, new items should only be incorporated into end products when the sourcing risk is managed properly. However, that functional view will not hold against the pressure to create and grow value-added end products.

Most innovations include newly developed components, and as a consequence there is a constant inflow of new bottleneck items. Moving a bottleneck item straight into the strategic category is not the optimal long-term sourcing solution. The challenge for the buyer is to ensure sufficient sourcing freedom for those items before their volumes grow. If the supply risk is managed down, the item will end up in the leverage box (the upper left-hand corner) or at least be to the left of the strategic category. An additional challenge is that this effort needs to be managed in parallel with building an effective relationship with the existing supplier of the bottleneck item. Additionally, in a number of cases these strategies also need to be managed against an agenda of exclusivity, and at a time when it is not yet possible to judge the market potential with any accuracy. Managing all of this requires a significant effort from the buyers, and calls for a sizeable amount of support from (among others) the technical and product management functions. The chances of success for buyers are significantly higher, the earlier they are involved in the end-product creation and development process.

For the selling side, more value is created in the right-hand side of the matrix. The sales effort is therefore normally focused on adding value components to ensure that the buyers (or end-users) perceive the item as carrying a higher supply risk.

If you look at a buyer's sourcing actions and tactics, it is possible to work out how they look at the item you have on offer, and where they categorize it in the Kraljic matrix. In many sales training sessions comments are made along the lines of 'I don't understand it. I'm frequently invited by many customers to take part in e-auctions, but these buyers don't seem to realize it's the wrong approach to take. My items are very special and you just can't do e-auctions against them because the other competitors don't offer the same. The buyers are comparing apples and pears.' These same buyers would probably argue that the salespeople are in a state of denial. They need to accept that to the buyer, their item rates as a generic commodity. Why does this gulf emerge? There are several possible reasons:

- Salespeople have started to believe their company's own marketing propaganda, and think their item is 'special', but objectively (as the market treats them as a commodity, so it is a commodity), it isn't.
- Sales and marketing communications have not managed to tell the value story right, so the buyer is failing to appreciate a real difference that exists.
- The item's 'special' characteristics might be important to some potential customers, but many others judge, rightly, that in their specific context they are not particularly relevant, and it makes sense for them to treat the item as a generic.

Once you understand where buyers classify your offerings, you should look critically at your sales portfolio. What is the unique selling point (USP) of the item, and is it one that genuinely matters to the customer, or just one that has been puffed up by product management or the marketing department? Does it justify a price difference (because it does indeed create extra value for the customer)? What communication strategy and other actions can you and your company use to ensure that buyers perceive a higher supply risk? (For example, there might be a way to make a generic item special by adding real value components.) You might need to accept that some items you offer have become more commoditized (in general or in a customer's specific context), and rethink how sales of the item should be managed.

In short, if you understand how buyers use the Kraljic analysis you can use it in your positioning of the item. Note that the emphasis here is on how buyers use it. It's no use doing your own Kraljic analysis and deciding how the item rates if buyers don't agree with you – although you can always try to find ways to make them agree.

For example, say a company sells an item that is used in some industries as a generic product. However, that same item could also be used in some niche markets in a much more specific way, as it has a special characteristic that rival generic products do not have. Perhaps your marketing people have focused on why the mainstream users buy it, and missed out on publicizing the USP. However, buyers in the niche sector will look quite differently at this item, and might give it either a bottleneck or a strategic item classification. It's to your advantage to pick up on this and sell the item accordingly.

A soup manufacturer decided to sell its soups in a lined paper carton, rather than a tin or packet. It sought suppliers for the cartons, and one company that had a suitable product reviewed the request to tender and decided that the customer's aim was to reduce its packaging price. It assumed the item was rated in the leverage category, and put in a quote that was competitive not just with other carton manufacturers, but with other types of soup package. However, it was quite wrong: the customer believed that the carton was something unique (as it was at the time; it has since become commonplace) that would provide additional value, and that it could position its product up-market of packet or tinned soups. It was not looking for a cheap price above all; from its perspective the item was in the strategic category.

What should you do if you realize that your buyers view an item as either routine or leverage, but you genuinely believe this is *not fair*, as the item is really very special? Here are some suggestions:

1. Do a real and honest assessment of the item's appeal to the market. Should buyers really perceive it as special, or if you are honest, does it not have any *real* additional value *for this customer*? (The acid test; if you were the customer would you pay anything extra for your product over

the competitors' products if you had to pay it personally?) If you still believe the item is more special than the customer perceives it to be, take steps 2 to 5. If not, accept that for this customer/item combination you are selling a commodity.

2. Ask yourself whether your company's sales story is clear enough about the real benefits. Are these benefits quantifiable, and could you prove them to the customer? One option might be to show the customer that you are willing to take a risk to prove that your item really can create additional value. You need to tailor the general story on the item's benefits to this item/customer combination.

3. Have you had a good opportunity for a discussion about your product's value (with the buyer and/or other functions in the buying organization)? If not, how can you create that opportunity? Could you achieve it by working on somebody else in the decision 'snail'? The buyer might not be the person most likely to perceive the difference that is the core of your special offering.

4. Is your sales team actually capable of telling the value story for this item, or have they responded to buyer perceptions and become focused purely on price levels?

5. Consider whether to decouple from each other items with different classifications in the Kraljic matrix. It is not easy to discuss items that are classed as strategic, bottleneck or even routine together with leverage items. The chances are that the discussion will default to leverage for all items, as the buyer will try to group it that way. From your perspective, it's better to ensure that all the products are seen as bottleneck or strategic items. But is that realistic? Remember to work within the restrictions laid down by local competition laws, but how can you effectively group your offerings?. It's worth trying to manage bottleneck and strategic items in a way that also gives you optimum results for routine or leverage products.

One company developed a 'procedure pack' that contained all the tools and disposables required for common surgical procedures (for example, an operation to remove a patient's appendix). The idea was that this would simplify life for theatre nurses, who tend to be under a lot of pressure, and enable them to avoid mistakes. If they could draw on a standard pack instead of taking the time to assemble one by one all the items that would be needed for the operation, they would save a lot of time (about 40 minutes between each procedure). More operations could thus be carried out in the same theatre, leading to overall lower cost and more income. The salesperson did an excellent job of explaining the benefits on the basis of detailed studies; all arguments could be proved by detailed financial analysis and were supported by thorough data on risks and time efficiencies.

The buyer then took out a calculator and did a standard costing for the pack by adding up the typical cost for each item it contained. This seemed to show that the procedure pack was a 'rip-off' as it was 15 per cent more expensive than buying the contents separately, and the only thing it offered in return was the box in which it was packed. From the buyer's point of view, this made sense. But when the salesperson managed to talk to the right stakeholders – those who would really benefit from the lower stress, the lower workload for theatre nurses, and most of all the fact that this simple offering would make it possible to carry out more operations in a single theatre – the salesperson was able to persuade them that the pack would more than pay for itself.

The case study is a perfect example of the need to find the right stakeholders and sell them the right story. Buyer motivation also played a part here. The buyer was probably working to targets focused on keeping purchase prices down, so it was no wonder that this superficially more expensive proposal was initially rejected on price grounds, despite the overall increased value.

To repeat, you cannot take it for granted that buyers will share your view of where an item fits in the matrix. If the buyer scores the supply risk higher, adapt your negotiating style accordingly. There are likely to be more opportunities to create additional margin on items with a higher supply risk, though they will vary from market to market. However, you must balance the opportunity for individual 'wins' with the need to build trust and a lasting customer relationship. You might win a battle (the highest margin for this specific item), but lose the war (by reducing the overall customer business opportunity). Try to ensure that negotiations are structured and items grouped in ways that fit the buyer's perception. If you understand the classification you can anticipate their tactical actions.

The Dutch windmill

The Kraljic matrix gives a good picture of how buyers look at an item from a commercial sourcing strategy point of view. However this is the buyers' view of the market for *their own* requirements and the financial impact for *their own* company. Obviously this does not necessarily have to be aligned with the supplier's view of the market and the financial importance for the supplier company. These different views on the market and its importance to the company might lead to a strategy, tactics and actions that could either support efforts at building a better and more effective relationship, or at worst make an effective relationship difficult.

To assess the importance of an item from a sales point of view, looking at the market and the customers, one way of classifying items is to map their current turnover (as this indicates the importance to the sales company) against their potential in the market (as this indicates future importance). This produces another two-by-two matrix (Figure 8.6) with the following four boxes:

- high attractiveness and low turnover – a development item;
- high attractiveness and high turnover – a core item;
- low attractiveness and low turnover – a nuisance item;
- low attractiveness and high turnover – an exploitable item.

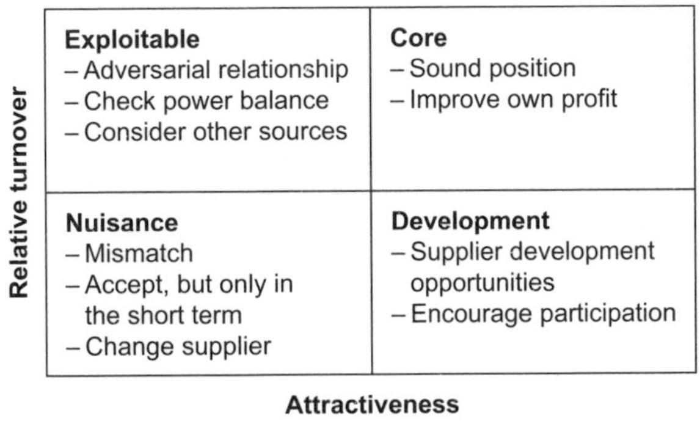

Relative turnover	**Exploitable** – Adversarial relationship – Check power balance – Consider other sources	**Core** – Sound position – Improve own profit
	Nuisance – Mismatch – Accept, but only in the short term – Change supplier	**Development** – Supplier development opportunities – Encourage participation

Attractiveness

Figure 8.6 Sales importance analyses

Purspective (a Dutch purchasing training institute, part of the Dutch buyers' association) developed a model that combined the Kraljic matrix for buyers with analysis from the sales side. They called the model the 'Dutch windmill' since this was what their diagram resembled (Figure 8.7). The original 'Dutch windmill' views the attractiveness of the entire customer portfolio rather than analysing the attractiveness at item level.

As the Kraljic matrix looks at sourcing strategies and tactics at item level (although indeed buyers will group them if it makes sense to them), an adaptation is made to the original model by also reviewing the sales attractiveness at the detailed item level rather than the portfolio level, understanding

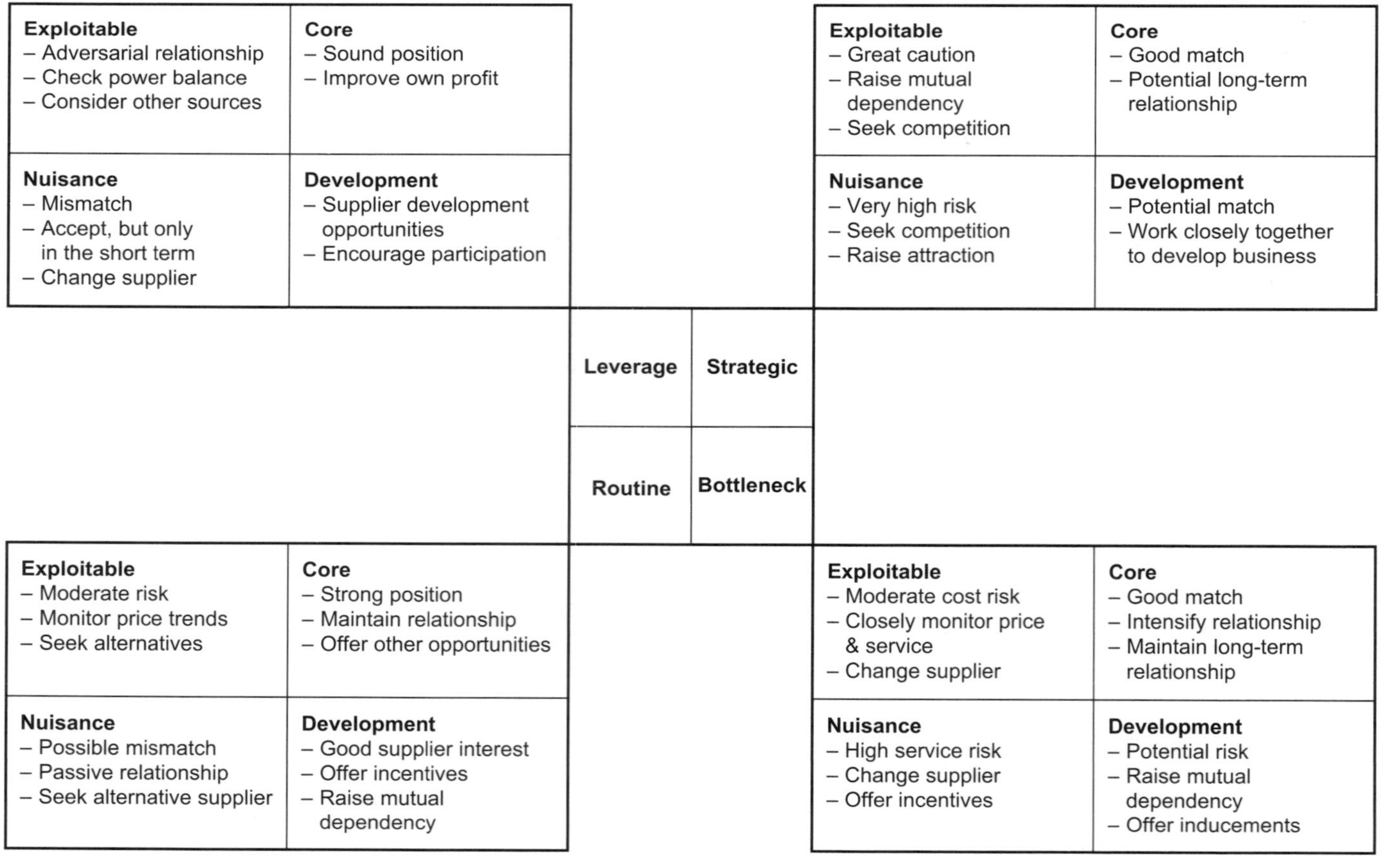

Leverage

Exploitable – Adversarial relationship – Check power balance – Consider other sources	**Core** – Sound position – Improve own profit
Nuisance – Mismatch – Accept, but only in the short term – Change supplier	**Development** – Supplier development opportunities – Encourage participation

Strategic

Core – Good match – Potential long-term relationship	**Exploitable** – Great caution – Raise mutual dependency – Seek competition
Development – Potential match – Work closely together to develop business	**Nuisance** – Very high risk – Seek competition – Raise attraction

Routine

Exploitable – Moderate risk – Monitor price trends – Seek alternatives	**Core** – Strong position – Maintain relationship – Offer other opportunities
Nuisance – Possible mismatch – Passive relationship – Seek alternative supplier	**Development** – Good supplier interest – Offer incentives – Raise mutual dependency

Bottleneck

Core – Good match – Intensify relationship – Maintain long-term relationship	**Exploitable** – Moderate cost risk – Closely monitor price & service – Change supplier
Development – Potential risk – Raise mutual dependency – Offer inducements	**Nuisance** – High service risk – Change supplier – Offer incentives

Figure 8.7 Linking buyers and sales analysis: adaptation of the 'Dutch Windmill'

that final decisions will always have elements of the overall attractiveness of the customer. In this way, each of the four classifications by the buyer (routine, leverage, bottleneck, strategic) can be matched by one of the four classifications of the sales analysis (development, nuisance, core, exploitable), giving in theory 16 different bases for a commercial relationship to be formed. Some of the potential combinations are less likely (although for seller and buyer to read the market differently is not at all uncommon), while others are potentially 'perfect' fits between the seller's view and the buyer's view of the buyer's side, so they could provide the foundations of a good relationship.

The different ways the buyer and the sales side look at an item can generate an effective relationship, an acceptable relationship or a relationship that is doomed to fail. If we take the Kraljic matrix in the centre of the picture as the lead, then the following overview develops:

1. *Buyer's routine items* generally create strong buyer positions, but as this category represents a limited spend for the buyer, there will be limited attention from the buyer for these items. Hence buyers will search for suppliers that will take over the 'hassle'. That behaviour in combination with:
    a) *A sales core item.* This could potentially create an effective relation at operational level if the sales side has the core skills to manage the buyer's total demand stream.
    b) *A sales development item.* This could work in a similar way to a sales core item, certainly if the development is around the full service. However don't expect the buyer's organization to spend a lot of time on 'joint' development, or willingness to be a test environment.
    c) *A sales nuisance item.* Unlikely to work. The buyer will not be willing to convince a supplier to continue this item, while the seller is not willing to give the item process the rigorous process attention required for routine items.
    d) *A sales exploitable item.* This is a potentially good combination, as the supplier will be keen to supply this item and has developed processes to do so effectively, but no further developments should be expected or required. Might not lead to the lowest cost chain.

2. *Buyer's leverage items.* As with buyer's routine items, the buyer has many sourcing options, but in this case is also willing to spend time on the process as it offers great returns. In behaviour in combination with:
    a) *A sales core item.* Major leverage will be applied by the buyer. The seller needs to sell, so all the pressure could be applied by the buyer. This will result in a very tactical relationship with 'hard' positions.
    b) *A sales development item.* A less likely scenario, because why should a supplier want to develop a 'commodity' product in a market that

already has significant supply options? However if it does so, the buyer's position is even stronger as the sales side needs to establish themselves in this market.

c) *A sales nuisance item.* This is a relationship mismatch and it is unlikely that this situation will actually exist. The buyer looks at the market as competitive, and therefore wants to drive leverage tactics. The supplier is actually thinking of exiting this market – and why not with all the pressure from all the buyers?

d) *A sales exploitable item.* While tactical deals could be reached in this scenario, ultimately this combination is liable to create quite a hostile environment, with a high chance that buyers will move their sourcing to another available supplier.

3. *Buyer's bottleneck items.* As with strategic items, the buyer will seek opportunities to reduce the supply risk. However with bottleneck items the buyer's impact is less, so this category might get less buyer attention, and hence gives more opportunities for the sales side to drive margins. In behaviour in combination with:

a) *A sales core item.* Takes away a bit of worry of the buyer: at least somebody wants to sell this and while it may be priced higher, given the impact on the buyer's total P&L, that might be less of a concern. For sales there is a good chance to get better than average margins or build a wider relationship. These two potential objectives require some careful balancing.

b) *A sales development item.* This creates a good basis for a collaborative relationship, as both the buyer and the seller have a mutual interest in developing this item and the players have a mutual dependency.

c) *A sales nuisance item.* This is a nightmare scenario for the buyer, as the item is required, while the sales side may stop selling it. Therefore if the sales side decides to continue supplying the item, this creates an excellent opportunity to drive better than average margins and potentially move the item to the exploitable category.

d) *A sales exploitable item.* The supplier has the upper hand here, but for the buyer security of supply is guaranteed. For the sales side this item creates interesting returns. The buyer will probably continue to search for alternatives.

4. *Buyer's strategic items* are key for buyers, with significant effect on their P&L. Hence they will try to build secure relationships. This behaviour with:

a) *A sales core item.* An excellent basis for a good relationship, potentially with the option to develop a very close one, resulting in a key account management structure.

b) *A sales development item.* Similar to the above, except that the buyer feels slightly more vulnerable. As a consequence buyers may be more willing to support supplier developments, but might in the mean-time look to alternatives as this item is so important to the company's bottom line.

c) *A sales nuisance item.* This position is extremely difficult for the buyer; the buyer will try to secure delivery from the current supplier, while in parallel a significant cross-functional sourcing activity will start. From the sales side, this situation might (as with bottleneck items) allow the item to move from nuisance to exploitable.

d) *A sales exploitable item.* If handled cautiously, this could form a basis for a reasonable relationship. The seller wants to sell but is harvest-ing the maximum return, probably without really investing any more in the item and the related supplier services. However, buyers might feel that they are not getting what they require, and so will try to create new suppliers for this item.

This overview clearly indicates how buyers and sellers can look differently at the same market and therefore have different strategies for the same item. As a consequence it is clear that aiming for a closer relationship with a customer is not always a route that will lead to success. The positioning of the item by a specific seller and specific buyer will determine whether a closer relationship is possible. Only when that basic condition is in place will the other elements required to build a relationship have an effect. Obviously relationship decisions are not based on the positioning of individual items but on the buying and sales portfolio. But even in that portfolio some items will therefore enhance the relation, while others do not add value (or even potentially undermine it).

Supplier portfolio management

Before we go into the supplier portfolio management process, it is important to understand how buyers assess the number of suppliers they need to man-age the business effectively. The optimum number of suppliers constitutes a balance between having all the possible suppliers in the mix to avoid missing an opportunity, and the understanding that working with a more limited number of suppliers will drive better results and is more efficient and effec-tive. The key considerations for the number of suppliers are:

- *Security of supply.* Buyers are generally very worried at the prospect of end-ing up in a situation where they cannot guarantee ongoing supplies. While pricing is important, they are very aware that internally their largest risk involves not price but availability. As a consequence, if the world was perfect (in the eyes of the buyers), they would have at least one other (than the existing main supplier) active supplier in the mix for all individual items.

- *Leverage.* Buyers want to ensure that more than one supplier is 'fighting' for a certain item. This gives them the opportunity to play the market, and allows them to have suppliers play different roles in the overall mix of supplier requirements.
- Management of each *supplier* is an *investment.* The level of investment needs to be balanced with the return, so the optimum point balances the number of suppliers that can be managed effectively and the required leverage against additional security of supply.

This optimum point will be different for different types of items with different characteristics. If a major joint development process is required to produce an item, it could be extremely difficult and costly to pursue this with more than one supplier. Therefore the buyer needs to find a way to create leverage and security of supply without having multiple suppliers lined up. In contrast, for a bulk commodity item, lining up several suppliers is quite simple and the cost of change is normally relatively low.

Generally buyers do not like to have just one supplier for an item or a category of items. While many companies use different terms for their supplier classifications, in general three types of suppliers can be identified:

- *Main supplier(s).* Such a supplier is frequently referred to as a (development) *partner, key* or *core* supplier – any term that indicates this supplier is responsible for major volumes and is closely involved in new developments. High delivery expectations are put on the partner(s), including a major focus on joint development and exclusivity, cost reductions, value creation and ongoing service efforts. In return the partner suppliers can expect a significant percentage of the total business from this customer.
- An upcoming supplier is sometimes referred to as the *challenger.* This supplier is lined up to become a main supplier for a category of items. It will get some of the customer's core business, but volumes are still relatively low, and delivery and services are followed up in quite some detail. The problem for this supplier is that it needs to live up to all the expectations and requirements of a partner supplier (and do even better if it is to move up in the supplier hierarchy), but has not yet been allocated the volume to do this cost-effectively. Moving into this position therefore needs to be seen as an investment in a move to the partner position. If this does not happen in the time estimated, this supplier should consider the investment lost and cut expenses, which will probably result in a rapid move back to being just a listed supplier.
- Other approved and listed suppliers are seen by buyers as *aggressors* or *support suppliers.* Such suppliers normally have small parts of the buying

portfolio, and the business relationship between buyer and seller is normally quite transaction-oriented, even somewhat opportunistic. Nevertheless they perform an important element in the overall supplier hierarchy, mainly because they represent the market situation to the buyer and therefore keep pressure on the partners and challengers.

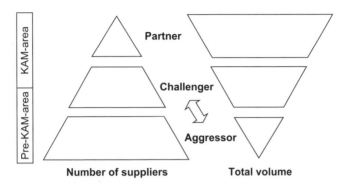

Figure 8.8 Supplier portfolio management

Figure 8.8 shows this schematically. The triangle on the left represents the number of suppliers, which is very limited at the partner level (typically one or two for a certain category of items or geographical area), slightly more at the challenger level (in a perfect world a ratio of two to the number of partners), with a manageable but wider group of aggressors and support suppliers. The triangle on the right-hand side represents the allocated volumes per specific supplier category. For the partner suppliers the volume is 50–70 per cent, 20–30 per cent for the challengers and 10–20 per cent to the aggressors. Higher in the hierarchy it is possible to move into a key account management relation (see Chapter 12 on buying relationships).

The division of the different volumes over the different supplier classifications and suppliers in each of the categories is not static. The make-up of the supplier portfolio will be reviewed regularly and will depend on market circumstances, the buying focus (value/cost or price), the current performance of the suppliers and several other supplier requirements (see also the section on supplier selection criteria in this chapter). In the aggressor category, suppliers will be exchanged more frequently or easily than in the challenger and/or partner categories.

The review process could be quite visible, with tender documents, presentations and multifunctional teams working with each other to select the best suppliers for each category. However, it could also be an ongoing classification process with ongoing input and feedback. The first move into a supplier classification model will normally be quite visible. Most companies carry out a more fundamental review every three to five years for their key items or when significant changes happen (such as changing technology, new or exiting key market players, acquisitions or mergers). In the years in between, there tend to be only small changes or different focus areas for review, through standard business review meetings with the supplier base. These interim reviews need specific attention from the salespeople, otherwise their relative positions might change without their fully appreciating this.

It is quite important for salespeople to understand which supplier categorization the customer is using, and what these categorizations really mean. First of all this should put the buyer's actions into a strategic perspective. Using its understanding of the supplier portfolio strategy, the supplier company can make decisions on where it wants to position itself (not all suppliers necessarily look to partner all customers, nor is it possible to only have partner customers). So this is a way of thinking consciously about what kind of supplier you want to be for *this customer*. This perspective also gives insights into opportunities and risks, and allows you to see the pros and cons of a certain position.

It is also important for the selling company to critically assess its real capabilities. Is it geared up to be a partner? Does it really have the innovation capability required, and the logistic processes to serve the customer where required? If it is a challenger, is the company (and not just the account manager) prepared to make the investment in *this* customer that will be needed if in time it is to become a partner? And if it is an aggressor, what exactly does it bring to the table? Is it simply offering volume, or does it have the capability to be a low-cost aggressor or a small niche supplier, or is it perhaps better positioned than other suppliers to deliver to a certain region? Why does the company want this customer in its customer portfolio? Most salespeople find it difficult to decide to walk away from a client, as they develop a sense of possessiveness about the account and their contacts, but these questions need to be asked regularly, and not only when the entire company embarks on a 'cost to service' exercise.

In markets where the buyer has a strong upper hand (normally commodity-type markets), you may find that after your company has been a successful key supplier for a few years, the buyer decides to reduce your volumes significantly (or even leave you out in the cold). Even if you do then manage to regain your former position, the buyer will look for improved terms and conditions. This is very frustrating for salespeople. They tend not to understand why they should have lost significant volumes when they feel they have been doing a great job for the buyer. In fact this happens because buyers believe that one of the ways to ensure ongoing competitive pressure for *commodities* is to change their main suppliers regularly. (Clearly for more supply-restricted areas this would not work.)

You might conclude from this discussion that all items have three levels of suppliers, but this is not the case. This reverts back to the Kraljic matrix, where the buyer can invest in building and managing a relationship with a supplier only for the bottleneck and strategic categories. For leverage items the buyer tends to buy more opportunistically, and run tendering processes regularly if and when contracts are due for renewal. A real partnership relationship is not likely to develop in the leverage or routine segments. Nevertheless do not be surprised if the buyer calls your relationship 'strategic'. The word 'strategic' in itself does not mean anything, but buyers have learnt that it seems to work well with salespeople. Sometimes companies seem to bypass hard economic logic when there is a hint that the relationship is or could be 'strategic'. The message here is to be cautious. It is advisable to check on the real intent of the buyer, and the additional benefits that you would get if the company were to move up the supplier hierarchy. Remember that the type of relation is linked to the type of products and the market circumstances, so unless you are a stationery supplier, you are unlikely to announce that you have a partner for paperclips.

Porter's analysis

Any relationship, any discussion, any interaction at any time between people has an element of power play. This is even more true in interactions that have an evident aspect of winning and losing, or give and take, as is the case with buyer–seller relationships.

Both buyers and salespeople need to be aware of their relative power. The Porter analysis is a well-known and useful tool to make the competitive playground very visible. The analysis maps the power of suppliers against the power of the customer, and analyses the effects of future power influencers through looking at new entrants and substitute products. Figure 8.9 summarizes this five-forces analysis.

The Porter analysis describes very well how buyers think on a day-to-day basis. Buyers will scan the market continuously for new opportunities, such as replacing a current purchase with a lower-cost item or one that will deliver increased value for the same cost. This happens regardless of their relationship with existing suppliers. Over the last few years this search has mainly focused on 'low-cost countries'. Many buyers have begun sourcing from developing countries, and have worked with suppliers there to help them get to a position where they can produce items at a better value/cost ratio than existing local suppliers. This opens up a new level of competition and therefore creates a new set of market dynamics.

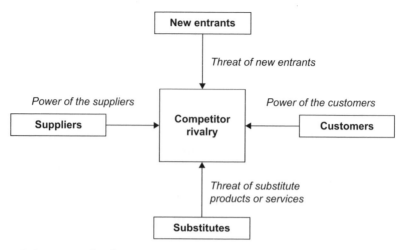

Figure 8.9 Porter's five-forces analysis

As the Porter analysis is such an established model, many organizations use Porter or derived models on their sales side to determine their own position in the competitive market. One common problem is that this analysis is done with a broad brush. It looks at the entire market – all product lines – or a large chunk of it, such as a specific important product line for an entire region. The analysis is normally carried out by a central group of product managers. Detailed customer-specific market information, which is available at the sales level, is frequently not taken into account. The analysis would better be done by looking specifically at customer usage, and not from the sales point of view but using a reverse-engineered view of customers. The new entrants and the potential substitutes might look quite different in individual cases than in an overall market assessment. Globally they might seem insignificant; locally they could present a real threat of replacement.

Another major problem, which is a form of denial, is to look only for the same items, instead of similar items or replacement items that could perform the same function but in a different way. Companies are then surprised from the 'left field' by a market that moves quickly away from a traditional solution. Salespeople often display this type of denial when they are confronted for the first time with a new alternative to their offering. They tend to focus on what the new offering does not provide that theirs does. Perhaps meanwhile their customer has tested the item thoroughly and concluded that although this is true, it nevertheless offers an improvement in cost/benefit terms. If you hear this from a buyer, you have two options. First, you can continue to insist that the customer is wrong, pointing to all the reasons you can find why your product is the better option. Sometimes, admittedly, this works. Sometimes buyers conclude that they have made a mistake; sometimes, indeed, they really have done. But in general your chances of keeping the business using this tactic are slim. And even if you are right and win the debate, you might have done major damage to the relationship. Someone in the buyer organization will have made the original call to change over, and especially if they are a key decision maker, they will resist a move back to the old alternative.

The second option is to work with the new environment. Find out in detail what the alternative item offers and why it is appealing to the customer, and try to find a way forward that will improve your position. This might include accepting that your offering is approaching the end of its life cycle and will only sell now if it is priced competitively with the new rival. Or it might be over-specified for this customer's usage and you could consider developing a better-fitting item at a lower cost, offering this as an alternative into the market. Or perhaps you can even find a way to sell the customer the new sourced item. But at the very least you should keep in mind this new knowledge in managing your other accounts.

It is crucial to understand what advantages and risks your item offers compared with the alternatives for each customer. When you are really clear about your power position in relation to a specific customer, you will be much better able to position your offering and to drive value where possible. Doing a power balance analysis for generic customers throughout the market will not lead to that insight; it is easier and cheaper than analysing all your important customers separately, but you will miss value opportunities for parts of the portfolio.

You should understand too that power balance is not an objective measure; subjectivity plays a large part. Both buyers and salespeople can use detailed preconditioning techniques to try to influence the other party's assessment of the power balance. The only meeting between a supplier and a customer without preconditioning is the meeting that did not happen (or at least, should not have happened, if it was you who did not use the opportunity!).

Supplier selection criteria

Many salespeople tend to believe that price (or at best cost) is the only thing that matters to buyers, even if they talk a wider agenda. While without doubt price is a significant driver of purchasing decisions, especially if the items have limited supply risks and are therefore on the left-hand side in the Kraljic matrix, elements other than price always have a (major) influence on the final sourcing decision.

Clearly it is crucial for sales professionals to understand the supplier selection criteria for any specific item at a specific time: not only those that are visible and shared with suppliers, but also those that remain below the surface. Supplier selection criteria are driven by a combination of many elements described in the previous chapters, such as:

- the customer's organizational set-up, including the purchasing maturity, the end-user/cross-functional integration into the purchasing processes and the internal customer decision power;
- the positioning of the item in the Kraljic matrix;
- the positioning of the supplier/item and relationship combination;
- the power balance;
- industry direction;
- market conditions.

While all of these play a significant role in the focus on suppliers and the delivery expectations about them, generically the overall selection criteria can be grouped into nine main elements. These nine elements need to really fit together seamlessly, and if one piece is missing the supplier selection process is incomplete. Emphasizing certain parts of the delivery requirements or expectations automatically means de-emphasizing other parts. Clearly the buyer is not the 'owner' of all elements. To make a complete picture, significant input is required from other functions, but the buyer is the key player who fits the jigsaw together into one picture that meets the overall requirements of the company at the overall lowest cost.

In the next few sections each element of the supplier selection criteria is explained. Clearly, industry and customer differences will add or cancel elements under each of the headings, but the general principles apply across all markets and items.

Base conditions

Base conditions are the 'rules' that the buying company strongly believes in (therefore they have a link to its culture), and in many cases they also link back to the mission statements of the company or its guiding principles. In principle base conditions are not negotiable and therefore not part of the 'give and take' or to be traded against any other criteria. They are fundamental to the buying company and therefore if a supplier cannot meet even one of them, it will not be qualified to become a supplier. Only in a few circumstances is a supplier selected even though it does not meet a base condition. For example, if new base conditions are introduced, existing suppliers might be given a grace period in which to comply with them.

A major food producer enforced a step change in the safety and quality agenda of all its suppliers. The new requirements were significantly above legal requirements and the usual industry standards. Suppliers were required to upgrade their facilities so that they could pass a quality and safety assessment by an external independent auditor. This called for investment as well as changed behaviour. Suppliers were given two years to meet the initial threshold, and expected to maintain a programme of constant improvement thereafter. It was made very clear that if the threshold level was not reached, they would lose all their business with the customer over a very short period. During the first two years progress was measured against a scale; after the two years was up, the question was simply whether the supplier met the new base conditions.

Other examples of base conditions are:

- a supplier working within a legal framework;
- the supplier working only with approved and audited subcontractors;
- base conditions on safety, health and the environment (see also the section on supplier selection criteria earlier in this chapter);
- (geographical) sourcing limitations, arising either from local law or physical constraints;
- financial stability requirements;
- fixed terms and conditions of supply (T&Cs) (although most T&Cs are negotiable).

Base conditions are not static, and may change over time as a result of changes in the company culture or external market influences. Any negative incidents that affect the customer, or one of its competitors, might have a major impact in leading it to set new and stronger base conditions. New management is another source of additional or changed base conditions, as a new management will have an effect on the company's strategic direction and culture. As a consequence, while the base conditions are not immediately negotiable, it is sometimes possible to influence them in the longer term.

Limiting conditions

Limiting conditions are requirements that are based on the strong views and preferences of the customer's buyers or other functional experts who play a part in the sourcing decision. These conditions are presented as quite firm in the communication process, and therefore salespeople often take them as non-negotiable (base) conditions. They are not and they can be traded off against other elements of the offer, although they will usually only be dispensed with in return for a significant benefit elsewhere.

Some of the examples mentioned above as base conditions form limiting conditions in other companies. Other examples of potential limiting conditions could be:

- the overall number of suppliers in the supplier portfolio;
- the mix of different types of suppliers;
- single versus dual sourcing guidelines;
- volume/turnover guidelines for individual suppliers (overall and by item, for example 'never let one supplier take more than 25 per cent of the entire supplier turnover' or 'never use more than 30 per cent of a supplier's capacity');
- maximum levels of change (for suppliers increasing or decreasing in relative importance, or the entry of new items/new suppliers).

Some companies might see almost any supplier selection criterion as so important that it is 'upgraded' to act as a limiting condition.

Depending on the focus, at a certain stage any of the selection criteria could become limiting conditions. If the company is short of cash, a limiting condition might be the supplier's payment terms. If a company needs to boost innovation, limiting conditions could be constructed around an innovation agenda.

As a consequence, the base and/or limiting conditions of their customers need to be reassessed by salespeople on a regular basis. They might find that a limiting condition becomes a base condition when a certain stage of supplier development is reached. It is important to understand the nuances of the differences between base and limiting conditions. Sales people should ensure they know why these conditions are imposed, and who exerts the key pressure for any of them. It is not always easy for salespeople to get the real story. Base conditions that during the process are not taken seriously by the supplier will be interpreted by the buyer as a sign of 'uncooperativeness' or 'lack of customer focus', while quoting on all requirements, including those that were less 'hard', might cause your quote to be uncompetitive. The ideal is to subtly try to test where conditions or requirements fall along the spectrum. How well you can do this will also depend on the relationship between the buying and selling companies. If there is a single contact point – one buyer and one salesperson – it is much more difficult to unearth this kind of semi-hidden information, and this means that the chance to respond effectively and successfully to the customer's needs is more limited.

Understanding the detailed requirements, where they come from, how hard they are and who is behind them (in other words, who is the key decision maker), should be a key focus point for every salesperson.

Culture

After base conditions and limiting conditions, the next selection criterion is culture. While it is only listed as the third of the supplier selection criteria, culture is arguably the underlying key success factor in a selection process, and is in some respects very closely linked to the base and limiting conditions. It is hard to make the cultural aspects of a commercial relationship visible, and even more difficult to make them measurable. Cultural misalignment between the selling and buying entities' objectives or execution processes will undoubtedly lead to major challenges in the relationship. While customer and supplier companies will both have their own culture, the level of cultural alignment and the synergy of the two cultures will be a 'base condition' for a successful business relationship.

The culture of a company could be described in many ways. Amongst other parameters, elements that are frequently seen as crucial for a successful business relationship are:

- the level of alignment (or misalignment) on the strategic direction;
- margin and growth expectations on either side;
- openness versus arms' length relationship;
- efficiency processes (level of drive for world-class performance);
- a 'go-for-it' or a 'why change' or 'not invented here' mentality;
- an opportunistic or an analytical marketing approach.

The challenge for this selection criterion is that it is so hard to describe what a corporate culture is, and how well two are aligned, let alone to work out what you should do and should not do to make a fit with a customer's culture. Cultural alignment does not mean having the same culture, and while many of a seller's and a buyer's objectives and processes could be very closely matched, other objectives and processes will differ. There is certainly a major subjective element to culture, and perception of it is inevitably coloured by the personalities of the individual corporate representatives that people deal with. However the culture of a company is more than the people representing the company in the buying and selling relationship. It will be affected by the countries or regions in which an organization operates, and by its ownership and structure (for example, a public company tends to have a very different feel from a family-owned company), and by its development over time, but none of these aspects dictate what the culture will be. Sometimes it doesn't even make sense to speak of *a* corporate culture, since in some multinational companies the culture varies from location to location, while other companies are extremely explicit in rolling out one company culture around the globe.

While it is not easy to change the culture of a company, this does not mean that it is static, and some key changes (for example, of ownership or leadership) could have major effects on the company culture over time. Interestingly, however, in spite of these disparate influences and its intangible nature, if you ask a varied cross-section of people about the culture of a company with which they all have dealings, they'll normally agree pretty well in their descriptions of it.

Cultures can strongly amplify the results or kill the opportunity to work together. No individual culture is wrong, but some conflicting cultures could cause significant problems in a commercial relationship. It is key for salespeople to understand the differences in cultures and appreciate how best to handle them. When they sense that it will be difficult to work with a customer because of problems in cultural alignment, this should have an impact on the decision whether to invest in the relationship. It is better to focus resources on customers where there is a good chance of success than to focus on customers that have a completely different view on how business should be run.

People

It may seem a truism, but people do make the difference, certainly in an important interface such as the selling and buying relationship. As with the cultural aspects of a company, many of the people aspects are hard to describe and even harder to measure. We all know how tricky it is to explain why we get on with one person and not with another, or why we judge them to be a 'good' or 'bad' type of person. But some aspects of the people agenda, such as organization, succession and educational level, can clearly be measured objectively.

Starting with the non-objective areas of the people agenda, an excellent account manager (that is, one the customer considers to be excellent) will have a significant positive effect on the customer's perception of the supplier, while an average or below-average account manager will destroy value, even if on objective measures the supplier is preferable to competitors. However, an account manager who is right for one customer could be the wrong one for another. This could reflect differences in corporate culture, or it could just be a personality clash.

A major misperception is that buyers rate account managers who always say 'yes' higher than those who sometimes resist their demands. The 'yes' people might make for less challenging exchanges, but when buyers are asked which account managers they regard as the best, and why, they often say something on the lines of 'It's sometimes difficult to get this person to agree to what we ask, but I like them because they really work on understanding our requirements. If they don't think something makes sense, they're prepared to say so. So when they do say yes, we know it will work.' Account managers who are capable of being proactive, coming up with ideas, and resisting customer behaviour that adds costs but no value, are generally seen as adding value.

It is important to buyers that the account manager can take decisions. Obviously buyers understand that major changes need to be referred back to management, but the account manager should have a reasonable degree of authority, and be more than just a person who conveys messages.

In many buying–selling relationships, another key interface is the technical contacts. Clearly here it is important that technical people visiting a customer understand its products and talk its language. Sometimes this means mastering internal jargon and specific ways of working that are unique to the customer.

The more subjective elements of the people agenda are:

- *Organization* – Key here is the set-up of the supplier: where do key people in the relationship report in the supplier's organizational hierarchy?
- *Education and training* – The key here is not the number of PhDs, but how up to date are the key interfaces between the companies on areas like technical know-how, the market and (supply chain) processes.
- *Succession* – Buyers rightly have very major concerns about this, particularly in small/family-owned businesses, where one or at best a very few people are driving the major part of the value the supplier can deliver, which forms the success of the relationship.

The people assessment score frequently has a major effect on other scores the customer gives the supplier, such as service, quality and innovation.

How can salespeople pick up customers' thinking on, or concerns over, the people agenda? On succession plans, customers often spell out their concerns, or at least ask questions that make them readily apparent. If they ask a question about, say, levels of education or understanding of their products, this might reflect an objective concern (particularly in a specialist or technical business where a degree of knowledge and understanding is essential), but it could also mask a more subjective one: perhaps they want to either work with or avoid working with a specific individual. In these circumstances it is wise to investigate further, trying tactfully to discover what the underlying concerns are.

Although there is so much that is subjective to the people dimension (as indeed there is to the culture one), that does not alter the fact that it is critical in building an effective relationship between the supplier and customer. Even if there is broad cooperation between different functions on both sides, most contacts normally involve a limited number of people, and making sure that all of these interfaces work effectively is a key attention point for salespeople and account managers, as it is for the buyers involved.

Service

Is service a differentiator or an enabler? In many markets with suppliers offering similar products and with similar to-market processes, service is a given and not so much a differentiator in the offering. On the other hand, buyers' expectations of the service level are sometimes different for their different supplier categories (such as partner, challenger, aggressor or support supplier). And some suppliers actually use service as a major differentiator. For example suppliers can reduce their support functions for commodities, and move ordering and order follow-up to the internet. They promote themselves as low-cost providers. (Of course, if their actual pricing does not fit this model, it will be a problem.) Another supplier might differentiate another commoditized product by adding services. For example one supplier of packaging moved to become a service provider by running the customer's packaging lines, using the customer's designs.

Service is crucial, whether it is an enabler or a differentiator. If service is 'just' an enabler (as some product managers say), failing to deliver is even more destructive, because a supplier without the right service will not get the business. If it is treated as a differentiator, a cost-competitive supplier giving less service might still be chosen for orders where the service is not an essential aspect.

Buyers tend to be far more concerned about service than they are willing to admit. Their internal reputation might suffer if a supplier fails to deliver on promises. The end-users will not fail to point out that it is not a bargain to get an item for 10 per cent less, then spend 50 per cent more on making the supply arrangement work. As a salesperson, you must appreciate how important this aspect is to the buyer.

Any service problems will affect not only the company's service rating, but also the rest of the selection agenda. They will also cause significant additional pressure to be put on the buyers, who will pass it on to you, often being quite confrontational, even when the relationship is not normally a confrontational one.

The service agenda tends to be a wide one. It does not only involve delivery on schedule. Other transactional service elements, accounts payable (invoice requirements), quality assurance and control (documentation, audit processes), R&D (service on development support) and other functions will also have specific and detailed requirements.

Examples of service subjects are:

- delivery (issues such as lead time, OTIFs (on time in full), expedited freight, delivery in non-standard modes or pack types);
- stock holding (which might involve consignment stocking, vendor-managed inventory, or vendor-managed and owned inventory);
- documentation (transport, certificates of analysis, import documentation and so on);
- service delivery, and whether it is reactive or proactive;
- innovation aspects, such as joint developments, or rights to first refusal of new developments;
- preferential treatment (over other customers);
- the ability to think 'outside the box', finding creative solutions.

Service is partly an objective requirement, with detailed measurable delivery data like OTIFs, invoice errors and lead time. However, a large number of the key service-related subjects are subjective and based on people's views. These subjective measurements relate to people and culture. Subjective measurements could be influenced quite significantly by conditioning the customer, spending time with the customer and aligning the selling organization to a wide spread of functions in the customer organization.

Being prepared for a discussion about service is crucial, especially if there are problems to be resolved. Buyers tend to learn quickly when things are not running smoothly. Not infrequently salespeople receive service information slightly later, because they tend to be more disconnected from the actual fulfilment process.

The way the supplier handles the challenges has a subjective impact on how the buyer rates the service, and this can be even more important than the objective measures. Buyers might think, for example, 'I know there have been real problems with delivery on time, but I have seen that they are on top of it and working through the root causes to prevent it happening in future. I know there might continue to be some problems in the next three months, but the way they acted shows that they are a very responsible supplier.'

If you as a salesperson proactively bring up any service issues you have learnt about (which means that you must make an effort to get up-to-date information), it could reduce their impact and, even better, could create a service-focused image for the company that outweighs short-term problems.

Costs

One of the key elements of the selection criteria is the costs. We have deliberately called this cost and not price, because it is important to ensure that the wider agenda of cost management is included in the analysis. In the selection criteria the subject is not just the pricing/costing offered, but how the supplier manages the costs and costing processes.

Cost issues include not just the selling price of an item, but how much it costs the supplier to deliver and how much it costs the buyer to handle. Costs are a key issue in the decision process because, as we have seen, the bottom line is a core concern and costs of inputs can have a major impact on it.

However, although the wider agenda must be considered, that does not change the fact that the purchase price is vital. It deserves significant attention, as market conditions might have significant effects on price levels. It is also important to understand what costs are included in the price of an item.

The heading of costs as a selection criterion covers not only the measurable costs (or price), but non-quantitative subjects related to costs such as:

- the supplier's pricing policy;
- type of costing (fixed or variable pricing);
- cost openness;
- track record on delivery of cost-reduction initiatives;
- the supplier's internal cost efficiencies (proven and also subjective assessment).

These subjective cost elements have clear links to culture (over issues such as how open about costs a company chooses to be, and its the pricing policy) and to proactiveness (which is linked to service, culture or even innovation), particularly for cost-reduction initiatives.

The message for salespeople is that it is critical to ensure they understand what the customer is looking for. Is the focus on price or on a wider concept of cost? It can help to consider the maturity of the purchasing organization, as described in Chapter 6. If it seems evident that the buying organization is looking at costs, questions of what they include and how to assess the costs arise next. Is this based on some other cost-management approach such as open book costing or joint cost-reduction initiatives? Understanding is one element in deciding the best way to structure the customer offering. If the focus is more on cost, significant attention should be given to getting a cross-functional understanding of the customer requirements.

Quality

Like service, quality is frequently more an enabler than a differentiator. Obviously any item must be of sufficiently high quality to fulfil the function for which it is intended, but there is less advantage (if any) in exceeding the customer's quality requirements.

The supplier selection criterion for quality has several elements. First of all, quality is linked to the agreed specifications and the ability to consistently deliver on them. This part of quality is normally very objective, and is measured in the buyer's vendor rating systems. It could be argued that this aspect of quality forms a part of the base conditions, as any supplier must be able to deliver against the required (minimum) quality requirements.

In addition to the objective, measurable quality aspects of delivery, most vendor rating systems collect views (and therefore subjective assessments) on how the supplier responds to quality incidents. This gives an indication of the customer's quality thinking.

A second part of the quality agenda is the ability of suppliers to upgrade or work with the customer on moving to new specifications or quality levels.

For new suppliers, where there is no history on quality performance, quality assessments (process audits) combined with quality accreditations are needed to provide a basis for predicting delivery quality. Most such assessments and audits use a scoring system, but the rating is largely subjective.

In summary, while quality has many objective, measurable elements, there is also an opportunity for the salesperson to influence the supplier's subjective quality image.

Sustainability, safety, health and the environment

A supplier selection criterion that has been added more recently involves sustainability, safety, health and environmental (SSHE) issues.

Many companies base questionnaires for their suppliers on the templates provided by influential organizations, for example the UN Global Compact (www.unglobalcompact.org/). Some also take into account specific sustainability stock indices, such as the Dow Jones Sustainability Index (www.sustainability-indexes.com/). Many companies have internal safety programmes aimed at improving standards, and they obviously want to ensure that the same standards are applied by their supplier base.

Many aspects of SSHE can be measured objectively, through questionnaires and detailed analysis. Customers' internal policies on SSHE can form base or limiting conditions, depending on the importance they give to this aspect relative to the entire supply agenda.

Innovation

Value could be delivered in two ways, by increasing benefits or reducing costs. This is true for customers as well as suppliers, and there is a constant tension between those who want to improve results through innovation and those who want to do so by cost reduction. The importance placed on innovation requirements depends on issues such as market circumstances and the life cycle of the customer's products. Buyers are not always in a good position to handle this agenda, and sometimes they find good reasons to downplay the importance of innovation. In general both innovation and cost management are crucial to deliver ongoing value (although different customer products at different times require different approaches). Sometimes the price/cost agenda and the innovation agenda might appear to be mutually exclusive, as companies tend to focus on one of them at a time, and leave the other to run as before. However, in any supplier selection process, particularly when it is cross-functionally driven, a judgement of the supplier's innovation capabilities is part of the overall assessment.

Because of these difficulties in judging future innovative ability, buyers tend to assess it by using a combination of historic performance and a subjective assessment of the people capability. This means that there is scope for the supplier to influence the judgement. Ways to achieve this include targeted marketing that features information on recent innovations, and customer-specific innovation processes such as innovation days, or inviting the customer's own R&D people to visit the supplier's R&D facilities.

Balancing the criteria

The nine criteria we have discussed need to be balanced to support the buying decision. In theory, base conditions are non-negotiable, and a supplier that does not meet them will be excluded from further consideration. However, real life tends to be more grey than black and white, and there is often scope for discussion, especially if none of the available suppliers meet the criteria, or just one player qualifies.

The other eight categories together determine the benefits of the supplier (relative to others); divide that by the relative pricing of the different contenders and the relative value of the suppliers is made visible.

Not all criteria will have the same weighting in this equation, and over time changes in the company's strategic direction might mean that different criteria are emphasized or de-emphasized. It is essential for the salesperson to pick up what the current key themes are.

It is important for salespeople to influence the supplier criteria by ensuring that the most weight is given to aspects where the supplier scores strongly. Particularly if your company is an established supplier, influencing the selection criteria could help to increase the barriers to new entrants. It is also important, of course, for the supplier company to work to meet the buyer's criteria, continually working to improve weaker aspects of its offering and further develop its stronger points. Suppliers that assess their own capabilities carefully are in a much better position to judge how customers will assess them. Doing this will avoid unpleasant surprises that affect your position as a supplier.

The seller's response...

How the buyer sees you is how you are – their perception is their truth. Some would advise that if you wish to please the buyer, behave as their perception implies you should behave. If they see you as a commodity (even though you know yourself to be a value-added supplier), behave as one, complete with price-for-volume offers. To do otherwise is to risk them ignoring you, or regarding you as a supplier with ideas above your proper station – ideas that would almost certainly come at a cost to them.

Such an approach might please them – it is always gratifying to have one's perceptions confirmed – but the approach comes with a risk: what if by pleasing them too well you dig your hole yet deeper, so postponing, perhaps indefinitely, the time when you can be seen as *you* wish to be seen?

There is no absolute answer to this dilemma – the best advice is perhaps to re-read this chapter and make sure that you fully appreciate the implications of the different ways in which buyers choose to position us. This will help you to read their behaviours better, and so identify the times when you must conform to their pigeonholed expectations, and when you might be able to argue your case for a different positioning.

In most cases, raising your status in terms of the Kraljic matrix is about going beyond the features of your offer in pursuit of genuine benefits, and then beyond that to finding solutions to the customer's most pressing problems. For the supplier of a physical product, this often involves wrapping services around that product. Remember, next time you are selling a product and services package, just why you are doing this, particularly if the services do not appear to add a great deal to your margins: if it is to raise your status, if it is to make yourself less dispensable, then make sure that you get the rewards intended.

The Kraljic matrix, and the Supplier Portfolio Management model both come with a health warning: buyers sometimes speak with forked tongues... This is not to say that buyers lie, but they may choose to tell a particular variant of the truth (for more on this see the following chapter).

The buyer may choose to tell you that you are less significant to the customer than you really are. This attempt to commoditize your offer is done for obvious enough reasons.

They may also choose to tell you that you are *more* significant than in fact you are, and in such a situation you are wise to be cautious. By stroking your ego (yours personally, or the corporate ego) they angle for favours, leading you to expect that such favours will be rewarded. By telling you that you are the only supplier they can currently consider doing business with, they are not telling you that you have carte blanche but rather that you should take particular care not to abuse your position and encourage them to look for alternatives – a scenario that often results in more generous treatment from the supplier than would have resulted from a multi-supplier arrangement.

The thing to look out for is where their words differ from their actions. You are a strategic supplier, you are told, and yet you receive standard bid packs from the administrators in the purchasing function. You are a commodity, you are told, and yet they want to see evidence of your logistics capability and examine your internal training pro- grammes. The greater the difference between words and actions, the more care you should take with the words – this is certainly a case where actions speak louder.

9 The negotiation game

This chapter is not intended to provide a full guide to negotiation techniques. There are a wide variety of books and an over-supply of courses that offer this. However a book on how buyers think and behave would not be complete without a chapter on this most visible and discussed aspect of buyer interaction with sales professionals.

As a result this chapter does not focus on all the ins and outs of the negotiation process. After a general introduction to that process, it describes what buyers think, how they play the game, what patterns they follow, and how a well-prepared sales professional can counter these tactics and therefore influence the outcome.

This book as a whole has tried to emphasize that the buying process consists of significantly more than a negotiation between a buyer and a seller. Nevertheless, negotiation is *the process* in which buyers and the sales professionals bring it all together. It is no good for either party to have carried out the right analysis, developed a great strategy and planned excellent tactics, but still to end up without a deal.

Sales professionals often complain that they do not understand the buyers' process and tactics. Even when they do think they know what the buyers are doing, they do not always understand why they do it. The next few chapters try to answer some core salespeople's questions, but first a number of key misunderstandings need to be cleared up.

Negotiation is a process, not a moment

Salespeople almost always say that negotiations with buyers are one of the subjects they would like to understand better. Then when you discuss it further with them, it is apparent that their focus is on the 'action': the process of sitting down and having a discussion with a buyer. However, this is only a part of the full process (which is described below). Negotiations are like a game of chess. You will obviously lose if you make a fatal mistake in the endgame, but most games are won or lost long before the endgame is reached.

In workshops when we discuss the negotiation processes with sales account teams, we ask them first when they last negotiated with their main customer. They usually reply 'During the annual negotiations, a few months ago'. Next we ask 'When was your last meeting with the buyer?' Usually the answer is, some time after this 'negotiation meeting'. This shows clearly how widespread the misunderstanding is that negotiations only happen during annual contract reviews. Negotiation needs to be seen in a significantly wider context, because every conversation between buyers and salespeople is a part of that process. (The good news, however, is that many buyers make the same mistake!)

Win–win is not always the goal

It is a huge misunderstanding if you believe that in all negotiations you should strive for a win–win outcome. Whether that is either feasible or practicable depends on the circumstances and the power balance between the buyer and seller. Figure 9.1 summarizes the playing field.

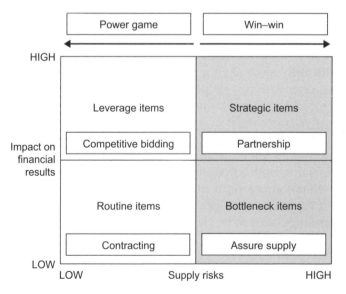

Figure 9.1 Win–win versus the power game
Source: adapted from van Weele.

This diagram uses the Kraljic matrix we described before. It is clear that it is only on the right-hand side that the buyer is looking for a 'win–win' outcome, as in that situation the buyer has more to lose than to win (because they see the company's dependence on the supplier as a risk for both price and availability). As a seller, you know that in these situations you can expect a win. On the left-hand side of the matrix, however, it is the buyer that is in the strong position. As a seller in this position don't expect a win–win process; it will be about how much you can afford to concede. Certainly for leverage items area the buyer will maximize their win, because there are many suppliers offering much the same commodity, and the buyer's task is to get it on the best possible terms. Buyers sometimes joke that they have reached the right deal if the sales professional starts crying. But see the next rule!

Never give something without getting something

Good negotiators will never give something without getting something else in return, even if what they get back is very small. There are two key reasons. First, whatever they gain will provide a better basis for the next discussion – and they could get a concession that is insignificant for the other party, but important for the own position. Second, to press hard for something in return gives a clear signal to the other party that the concession you have made is a real sacrifice. Perhaps objectively it is not (although often it is), but either way, this makes the buyer feel they have won an important point.

Obviously there are different negotiation styles, but ultimately all negotiations are based on finding a mutually acceptable compromise between the best possible outcome for each player, and the 'walk-away' point: the worst the player is prepared to accept. Both sides of the negotiation game are trying to find the other's walk-away point. If you make a concession without pushing for something in return, the signal you give is, 'I'm a long way away from my walk-away point,' and this will trigger a push for further concessions.

In preparing for a negotiation, it is therefore key to understand (you should be able to list) which concessions you are prepared to make, and what you might try to obtain in return. (Then, you need a strategy to play your hand so that you maximize the outcome.) This links to the next point.

Preparation will determine success

We all know people that regard themselves as 'smooth negotiators'. They walk into a discussion without any preparation, relying on their gift of the gab to get them through. And that is what they do: get through. They carry out 'damage control', not knowing what they want to achieve, only what they do not want to lose. This means they will lose some points, and they won't make real gains in return. The key message for negotiations should therefore be:

Failing to prepare is to prepare for failure

We all have done this. When you are really busy, needing to do too many things at the same time, you might feel it's a small miracle that you even manage to turn up for the meeting, and there's no chance that you sat down and considered what you wanted to achieve in advance. But in this case you have to leave the initiative to the other party, who all too often proves to have prepared very well. Unlike you, they know everything that has happened in the market and have reviewed everything that has been discussed in previous meetings. From their first move onwards, you are on the defensive. At best you might, with a lot of sweat, maintain your existing position. Perhaps at the end of the meeting you get them to agree to a second meeting, and finally in a third meeting you make a deal that 'didn't cost you too much'. But this process will leave you uncomfortable: you know you didn't get a good result and you don't have a good feeling afterwards.

Most of us have experienced the opposite too. We've had the chance to prepare, and taken it. We come into the meeting clearly understanding our side's strong and weak points. We score a few points early in the game and never lose our head start. We close the meeting, fighting off any suggestion for a follow-up or deferral, with 75 per cent of our best-hope agenda agreed. We go back to our office and silently shout *'YES!'*

Good negotiators do not lie, they tell a 'version of the truth'

Telling a straight lie in negotiation is a risky business, and good negotiators do not take that route. This is especially true if they know that this is only one stage in a long process of negotiation: perhaps prices are being agreed for the next six months, after which there will be a review. However, not lying does not mean telling 'the truth, the whole truth and nothing but the truth'. Some people feel the need to tell their counterpart things they have not even been asked, but good negotiators select what they want to share (and how), and also specifically decide what they do not want to reveal.

For example, a buyer might tell the account manager from their current supplier that they have been testing an alternative material from another supplier, that it has passed laboratory approval and that they are now in the next phase. It would not help them to admit that the full-scale plant trial has failed miserably, and there's no prospect of making the switch just yet.

Negotiators need to try to uncover this kind of information, the things that the other party would prefer not to reveal. The trick is to ask more questions, especially during what we call the 'diagnostic and conditioning phase'. Too many people listen to a message and jump to conclusions. Smart negotiators know that, use it to control their own revelations, and also try to avoid those premature conclusions and force more revelations from the other person.

Negotiation skills need constant maintenance

Since it is such a critical process in finalizing the deal, it is surprising that both buyers and salespeople do not take regular steps to maintain and improve their negotiation skills. Perhaps you went on a good training course on negotiation skills 10 years ago, and you've been handling negotiations frequently ever since. That does not mean you can take it for granted you're doing as well as you could. You might think your technique is pretty good, but then you never see what it looks like to an objective observer. All people have their own styles and habits, and they tend to be amplified over time. We all need to review what we're doing regularly.

In the next few sections, we focus on some of the key elements of the negotiation process. Specifically, we look at how trained negotiators could use the entire process to reach their targets. First there is a brief high-level view of negotiations as a process rather than an action, how this process could help to influence salespeople, and how they can counter buyer tactics. Next, linked to the analysis buyers perform, we try to capture a number of key elements in the interaction between buyers and sellers. Finally we explore the power balance and key standard purchasing negotiation tactics. Understanding all these key elements of negotiation will help to give you a better outcome from this critical process.

The negotiation process

The overall negotiation process can be divided into three major sub-processes:

- the diagnostic and conditioning process;
- the negotiation meeting process;
- the implementation and 'aftercare' process.

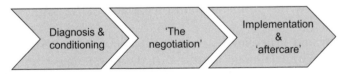

Figure 9.2 Negotiation phases

Each of these processes has specific characteristics and targeted achievements. It is important to understand that although we use this breakdown to analyse the process here, in practice the stages form a continuum. Implementation and aftercare need to run smoothly into a conditioning process for a new negotiation cycle. An even more important point is that good aftercare is probably the best way to condition the buyer for the next cycle.

The diagnostic and conditioning process

The diagnostic and conditioning process is the most critical phase, as it is the preparation phase for the entire process. It will determine a significant part of the outcome. This phase basically has two main deliverables: first, to carry out a detailed diagnosis – basically a situation assessment – and second, to 'condition' the other party to the expected outcome, including testing some ideas.

The *diagnosis process* focuses on information gathering. You should review all relevant facts, feelings and the views, rational or otherwise, of both parties. This is also the time to explore opportunities and understand the other party's key challenges. You need to understand the required outcome for both parties, and this normally starts with listing your own organization's needs. This might sound easy, but in reality those needs are frequently not clear and some could be contradictory, which is clearly not a very good place from which to start a commercial discussion.

While listing your own organization needs has its challenges, listing the buyer's needs is even more difficult. The needs could be either upfront or hidden. Even spoken needs could be 'just' preconditioning steps rather than real needs. An example of this is a buyer saying: 'We need to reduce the costs.' The buyer might really be desperate for a price reduction, or might just be trying to influence you prior to the negotiation meeting.

Needs that are not expressed can sometimes be picked up through hints given, but this is always difficult. Among those that are normally hidden are the buyer's personal needs. For example a buyer who knows they are close to a promotion might avoid risk by saying 'I'm not prepared to change over to the new specifications right now.' If you understand that this remark is driven from personal 'hidden' requirements to avoid taking any risks at that time, you might help the situation forward by taking away the risk and still seek the change. As another example, a buyer might be under a lot of pressure because their organization is unhappy with the existing service. The buyer might be anxious to resolve the problems almost regardless of the cost.

Both hidden and articulated needs might come from other parts of the organization. The challenge here is that the buyer might not be entirely committed to them, but will be under internal pressure to deliver on at least some of them. A salesperson needs other contacts in the buyer organization to be able to pick up and assess these needs. Their likely success will depend on the sales penetration into the customer's 'snail' (see also Chapter 12 on buying and selling relationships).

Buyers' needs can be analysed into three classes: 'must achieve', 'would like to achieve' and 'would be interesting to achieve'. 'Must achieve' issues tend to be driven by internal pressure, while the 'would like to achieve' issues represent more the buyer's personal agenda. 'Interesting to achieve' items might represent an opening position, but not necessarily something the buyer expects to deliver. It can happen that the 'would like to achieve' agenda is less ambitious than the 'must achieve' one: this happens when buyers feel they are being pressed to deliver something unrealistic. Buyers tend to behave irrationally in this situation.

Another part of the diagnosis process consists of assessing the power balance and analysing the strengths and weaknesses of both parties. Assessing who will be involved in the negotiations, understanding their behaviours, techniques and styles (and particularly their weaknesses), is a very useful preparation.

For simplicity we are discussing diagnosis as part of the conditioning and preparation phase, but clearly when the customer shares (or reveals) new information at any point in the process, it needs to be analysed and put into perspective.

The next step is to choose a negotiation tactic based on the total inventory of the needs, views, feelings and styles of the two parties. Part of that tactic might be a heavy preconditioning process.

Influencing the starting position of the other party prior to the negotiations is very important, and will probably determine over half of the outcome of the negotiations. You can achieve this by making casual remarks, stating your expectations (informally or formally), or applying some pressure (open or hidden). Part of this influencing game could be even a so-called 'pre-lock-in'. This is a tactic where even before the negotiations begin, one party spells out some minimum requirements. This can be done by buyers or by salespeople.

The key elements of the conditioning phase are summarized in Figure 9.3.

- Explore
- Understand
- 'Pre-lock-in'
- Influence
- Identify opportunities
- Find weaknesses/ strength/threats opportunities/
- Build relation

Figure 9.3 The negotiation process: the diagnostic and conditioning phase

Because preconditioning is so important, let's look in some depth at a few examples.

I'm sure you understand that for next year I've had to set my budget in line with the market circumstances, and therefore I expect you to follow that.
A sentence like this could set expectations and boundaries to what you can do later in the negotiation process. Buyers will only make this remark if they consider the market to be weak. This is a bottom-up lock, and it sets expectations: hearing this, a salesperson is going to be uneasy about proposing to increase prices.

From now on we expect our suppliers to support us in managing our cash flow better. Therefore all our contracts will have a minimum 90-day payment clause. I'm sure you will not have a problem with that.
This is an attempt at a classic pre-lock-in. It tries to decouple the pricing discussion from the terms discussion.

I do understand your situation. However, because you are such a key supplier to us, I expect you to work constantly on our behalf to reduce costs. I must say that I'm somewhat disappointed with productivity delivery from you over the last year.
This is clearly both a threat (a power play to test the power balance) and an attempt to find weaknesses in the other side's position. No one wants to start a negotiation from a weak position.

Our new CEO is really changing the game. He has announced a major cost-savings project and this will have an effect on how we will do business. You can make both of our lives significantly better if you find me some real cost savings before the next meeting.
This tries to influence the starting position. It takes a change in the company as almost an excuse. The message is 'If I'd been in control I wouldn't have done this to you, but in the circumstances you need to perform.'

The salesperson too can try this kind of tactic, especially using the market situation:
I'm sure you too have noticed that the crude oil price has gone up quite significantly. The main producers are short and at the moment we are in a process of defining which customers we can continue to supply, as we are fully sold out.
The main challenge is to recognize attempts to create a pre-lock-in and a preconditioning statement. When you identify them, make sure that you ask for further explanation, to test the 'hardness' of the points. Is this a real constraint, or just an attempt to influence you? In most cases it makes sense to refer back to this kind of remark shortly after the meeting in which it is made. This gives you the chance to dispose of them before the 'real' negotiation meeting starts.

The negotiation meeting process

After all the checking of opportunities, understanding the options, challenges, understanding your own and the other side's position, understanding external factors and so on, the day comes when you sit down to what is understood by both parties as 'the negotiations'. Obviously in most cases this part of the process will take several meetings, possibly with phone calls in-between (either to negotiate, or to try to influence the discussions). The phases are often not clear cut, and some aspects of the deal might remain in the conditioning phase while other parts have already moved into the negotiation phase.

The aim at a real negotiation meeting is to reach an agreement in detail. In principle it is a formal discussion in which both parties understand that they are trying to reach a certain outcome. Based on the conditioning phase and the level of preparation by both parties, it is likely that all those at the negotiation table will have objectives. They know what they would like to get out of the discussion. They have also probably made a list of what they can give away in the process. This setting of 'wants' and 'gives' depends largely on the outcome of the previous phase, hence the importance of spending sufficient time on the conditioning phase and on assessing the information it provides, before starting the 'action'.

The main elements of the negotiation phase are outlined in Figure 9.4.

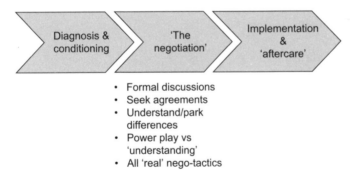

Figure 9.4 The negotiation process: the negotiation phase

There are many ways of handling a negotiation, and later in the book we show examples and discuss tactics. In general a negotiation phase focuses on reaching an agreement. This normally means finding an acceptable solution: not necessarily one that both parties are happy with (that would be a true win–win scenario), but one that both parties say yes to.

The main factors that will influence the discussions are the setting and 'tone' of the meeting, the negotiation style of both parties, which includes the way they try to reach their preferred outcomes, and how the parties have prepared for the meeting. Normally at the start of the negotiation discussion it becomes clear very quickly that there are a number of commonalities but also a number of differences. The fact that there are commonalities should encourage people to try to resolve the differences. How that is done will depend on many factors. One way of getting to an agreement is for the parties to be willing to listen to each other's arguments, which tends to deliver a more balanced solution as people move towards a settling point. Another way is a process of power play in which one party makes demands of the other.

The elements for running a negotiation meeting that it is important to plan for are the:

- style;
- roles;
- setting;
- timing;
- process for settling differences.

Style is about the personal 'comfort' style of the people around the table. Different negotiators have different personal preferred styles. We can analyse them into five major types

- competitive;
- collaborative;
- avoidant;
- accommodative;
- compromise.

Being able to move between styles enhances the impact of the message. While everybody has a personal favourite, styles should be varied during the discussion, depending on the required outcome. Good negotiators have the ability to be actors. Someone whose base style is collaborative but who changes in the meeting to a more competitive style will have a significantly greater effect than a person who is known always to be competitive. The key is to be aware of your own personal style and train yourself to move between different styles.

If the discussion involves more than one person from either side, it is important for the representatives to agree the *role* each of them will play. Their objectives need to be aligned, and so do the messages they both send. Avoid letting more senior representatives overrule their juniors; this will be interpreted as a weakness in the position and therefore an opportunity.

A buyer will often be very happy if the direct boss of the sales account manager is brought into the negotiations. Buyers often say they make their best deals in such circumstances, as the managers frequently devalue the sales professionals and are willing to make compromises they would fire their subordinates for. For someone at a more senior level to join the next meeting is generally an excellent tactic for getting bigger concessions, but this does not happen if there is not good coordination between the players.

The *negotiation setting* is the next point of attention. Clearly in some political negotiations (peace treaties and the like) the negotiation setting is itself something to be negotiated, with important discussions on where to meet, who will participate, how they are to be seated, the agenda (and more important, what will be not discussed) and so on. Of course normally in business discussions this is less of a challenge, but thinking through some of these issues could be helpful in achieving the required outcome.

Should the meeting be held at the buyer's or the seller's premises? Most people think there is a small advantage for the home player, but this depends on the focus and aim of the meeting, the general relationship, the style of the negotiators and many other factors. Sometimes meeting on neutral ground is a key enabler for a successful outcome.

Give some thought to the seating arrangements: for example with people confronting each other across the table, or people from both sides alternating around it. To interleave the delegations sends a more cooperative message but can create communication challenges.

Although there are a number of tricks with setting a meeting, such as seating one side to look into the sun or using chairs of different heights, they rarely produce significant benefits and can come across as counterproductive game-playing. But planning the setting of the meeting well could be a major enhancer.

Timing in negotiations is also important. Timing has three aspects:

- when to hold a meeting, and if there are to be a series of meetings with different suppliers over the same contract, in what sequence to meet them;
- timing of messages in the meeting;
- timing of the length of the meeting.

When to hold the meeting depends on time pressures (such as decision timelines and planned deliveries), market pressures, type of products and many other issues. The sequence of potential suppliers again requires some thought. For buyers it is normally beneficial to start with new suppliers before seeing the current supplier, as this will probably increase the pressure on the latter. Last but not least, depending on the people involved, early morning meetings, afternoon meetings and dinner meetings create different atmospheres.

Timing of messages in the meeting is more difficult to manage and to prepare for, as no discussion can be fully scripted in advance. However if you take some time to prepare not just what needs to be said but in what order, you are likely to convey a stronger message.

The last element of timing is extending the meeting or reducing the time available for the discussion as a whole, or of a certain subject during the meeting. Again, preparation is useful.

The implementation and aftercare process

Assuming that parties reach an agreement at some stage, the last step in the negotiation process should also get sufficient attention, as it ensures *implementation* of the agreement. It focuses on *negotiation aftercare*, which is critical both for a successful implementation and as a preparation for the next negotiation process cycle. This third step therefore closes the loop to the first step, the conditioning process. It is the most undervalued part of the negotiation process, and both buyers and sales professionals have a tendency to move on and give it insufficient attention.

It starts with a clear milestone: the closing of the negotiation discussions. Both parties understand that they have reached agreement. A small recognition (or celebration if it is a significant agreement) marks the official closing of the negotiation process. Sometimes a handshake is all that is needed, but this may also involve signing a formal contract.

Now that the parties have reached an agreement, the details of what is agreed needs to be written down. Sometimes the mechanics of the negotiation discussion mean that this requires some renegotiation or clarification to get the exact agreement on paper. This could lead to some issues being reopened, but normally the process runs pretty smoothly.

Now that the preconditioning phase, the negotiations and the contracting are complete, the parties need to focus on getting the contract implemented. This is an important separate step: it does not come automatically with the signature of the contract. Making the deal work requires communication both internally and between the parties.

Last but not least is the process of aftercare. In most situations the contract will be open for renegotiation after an agreed period (which could be a month, a year, or three or more years), so it is good to understand the scars the negotiation left on the other party. During this process, which is normally very informal, a good negotiator will already be starting to precondition the other party for the next review phase.

Figure 9.5 summarizes these implementation and aftercare phases.

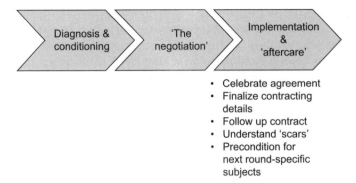

- Celebrate agreement
- Finalize contracting details
- Follow up contract
- Understand 'scars'
- Precondition for next round-specific subjects

Figure 9.5 The negotiation process: the implementation and aftercare phase

As an example of how aftercare shades into preconditioning, a buyer might comment: *'I'm really happy with this new contract, but I've had a hard time selling it internally. What went down worst was the compromise I made around the new stockholding levels without financial compensation.'* The salesperson will note immediately that the buyer is claiming to be, and perhaps really is, scarred and under pressure, and that stockholding levels are likely to be brought up at the contract renewal phase. If you get the sense that the problem is sufficiently serious to perhaps jeopardize the contract working, it might be useful to signal a willingness to keep the issue under review. You could say, for example, *'I appreciate this was a difficult point for your company to accept. I believe we now need to focus on implementation, but let's agree to review the situation in six months' time.'*

The negotiation power balance

The tone and style of negotiations is very much dependent on how people perceive their relative power (unless one of the negotiators is the kind who always goes for the 'kill'). In theory both parties should read the power balance similarly, as could be expected if during the diagnosis and conditioning phase both carried out a good inventory of the market (for example using Porter's five-forces analysis) or a high-level SWOT (strength, weaknesses, opportunities and threats) analysis. The buyers might also have used a Kraljic analysis (or similar) and the seller would have looked at the importance and potential of the item for the sales portfolio. But in reality both sides might come to quite different conclusions. Factors that cause this include a different definition of the market, a different view on competing technologies or new supplier entries, and a lack of full understanding of either the item offered or the way the customer uses it (that is, the value delivered to the customer).

Therefore quite frequently during the diagnosis phase and sometimes even during the core negotiations, the parties are surprised by each other's positioning. This will certainly be the case if signals sent during the conditioning phase have not been picked up well or have been interpreted incorrectly.

A negotiation power balance will also have a timing element. If the buyers feel that the power is always on the selling side, for example because the supplier is the single source, they will push internally for a reformulation or to build up a second source, perhaps from outside the industry. On the other side, if the sales side sees all buyers as achieving better and better terms, they might decide to move their focus and cease to target some market segments and offerings.

In short (see also Chapter 8 on the Kraljic matrix), the supply situation is not constant and is not the same for all suppliers and customers. It needs constant updating.

Negotiation tactics and buyers' tricks

There are many negotiation tactics that experienced negotiators can use, and the examples given can and will be used by both experienced sales professionals and well-trained buyers. The chapter is written from a buyer's point of view, but obviously sales professionals can use the same tactics to get their required results.

Although a number of tactics are discussed here, the list is not exhaustive; it just covers some frequently used tactics. The tactics tend to focus on achieving one of the following objectives:

- changing the power balance;
- creation of confusion to cause uncertainty;
- pushing for a concession.

Sense of urgency – time management

Buyers might play with time in several ways. They might suggest a meeting at very short notice (increasing pressure) or delay one, especially when it is not in their interest to make a new agreement. They might arrange a very short meeting, so that not all subjects can be discussed or to push for a quick concession, or plan a very long meeting (without informing the salesperson in advance) and use it to push repeatedly for a concession.

It is sometimes is in the buyer's interest to delay a discussion or delay making decisions. This is predominantly the case when a discussion or a decision/compromise would lead to a worsening of the terms and conditions. Examples of delaying tactics are cancelling meetings, claiming to be unavailable for a meeting, requesting more information (for the purpose of winning time), and pretending to be 'not the right person to discuss this with'.

You might think that this kind of gamesmanship will not prevent the inevitable happening, but it does repay the delayer. If at the beginning of a budget year the salesperson wants a price increase of 4 per cent, and the buyer is able to delay the agreement (and therefore implementation) by one quarter, the impact that year is reduced to 3 per cent.

Similarly buyers sometimes try speed up the discussion process by building in price and time pressure, for example by giving the supplier an extremely short time to prepare for a meeting, or asking for a decision on a proposal they have made very quickly after a meeting. These tactics are normally only used when the buyer already has a significant advantage in the power balance.

Time management tactics can also be used to change the power balance, add confusion and possibly push for concessions.

Good guy–bad guy

The 'good guy–bad guy' tactic is a classic approach that is frequently used when the meeting is attended by more than one representative from one or both sides, but it continues to be effective. It makes it possible to put across a tough message (from the 'bad guy') and also to be conciliatory and work to preserve the good relationship (by the 'good guy').

The standard set-up is that one person is aggressive, makes the difficult demands, and is at times unrealistic or even abusive, while the other plays the more understanding person. The good guy gives the impression of being reasonable, willing to bridge the gap, on your side and even apologetic for the behaviour of their colleague. This puts a lot of pressure on the other side to make some compromises to the nice guy. This tactic is focused on power balance changes, but adding a bit of confusion is often a useful side effect.

Lock in price – increase value

Obviously before a price discussion starts, there has been a discussion of the specifications and requirements for the item. The buyer will try to understand the extra costs for additional requirements or options as well as the price deductions for a reduction in the scope of the item. One of the tactics then used is to agree a price for a lower specification, and to try subsequently to increase the scope of work without incurring additional costs.

For example, a buyer of a machine tool might agree the price then ask the seller to add in the training of operators, translation of manuals and free spare parts. This tactic is called 'lock-in price – increase value'. It is predominantly a tactic that is linked to concessions.

One-off/special favour

This is a standard tactic. The buyer is trying to understand the flexibility in price setting, and challenges the seller to give a better price 'just this time'. A special reason is given, and the seller is put under pressure to agree, but the discounted price sets a precedent for the future. You should be wary of any requests on these lines.

The buyer using this tactic says something like 'I do appreciate that your usual pricing is fair, but I really need you to try to give me a lower price for this particular order.' Often the follow-up carries a hint of an opportunity – the buyer hopes to place more business in future, wants to make you look good in an upcoming supplier review – or a threat: if you don't agree, the buyer will look for quotes elsewhere. A variation on this theme is: 'I just don't have the budget.' In this case the buyer tries to turn their problem (if it actually exists) into the salesperson's problem.

A considered approach to this tactic is important. Refusing to set a precedent might hurt the relationship and cause the buyer to carry out their threat. On the other hand, as the special deal will prove to be less special in the next round of discussions, only agree if you have already decided that this customer is worth it.

To avoid linking a one-off agreement to prices in the future, you might consider attaching a special condition to the special price. This might involve the buyer's performance, such as hitting a certain volume of turnover, or instead of the price concession, offering a special rebate at the end of the contract year. Buyers tend to start the next round of discussions from a net level, though, so this could have only a limited effect. You'll get a response like 'The market is so tough that we really can't go back to the previous price now. I'm relying on you to agree on this price for another year', or simply a bald statement that as far as the buyer is concerned, the last price paid represents the market level.

The one-off/special favour is clearly a tactic focused on pushing for a concession.

Magnify small negative issues

Bringing up small problems over the previous period is a well-known tactic for influencing the opening negotiating position. Obviously service and quality issues need to be discussed, and it is important that parties share these openly with the aim of learning from them and improving performance. However, as a negotiating tactic, this is not about improving service or quality, but targeted on putting increased pressure on the negotiations.

The buyer says something like 'I understand that you have some costs issues. However, I think you need to manage your service better before I'm even prepared to listen to any of your arguments', or 'Our managers were very unhappy when that delivery arrived a day late last year. They haven't forgotten it. It caused serious problems with one of our main customers.'

Usually this tactic draws on genuine service-related issues, but the buyer magnifies them and exaggerates the effects. The challenge to the salesperson is to judge the complaint against the tactics: is there serious dissatisfaction, or is this just a negotiating ploy?

'Magnifying small negative issues' is clearly trying to change the power balance. The salesperson will feel uncomfortable driving a hard deal in the face of buyer grumbles on other issues.

Cost-based arguments to lower the sales price

Buyers are trained to think that price is in principle 'cost plus margin', unless the market circumstances dictate a lower price (giving the seller little or no margin). This market logic tends to work in only one direction: market circumstances are seen as a reason for the seller to accept a lower price, but not a reason for them to charge a higher one when they have the power to do so.

Buyers who use this tactic will start by guessing at the seller's costs (including overheads) and adding on what they believe is a reasonable margin. Typically they share these calculations. If you see that they have allowed too little for overheads, they will return the task to you by claiming the figure is reasonable, and if your firm's overheads are higher they need to be brought down.

As a consequence, when the seller would like to discuss prices, buyers automatically shift into a discussion of costs on the supplier side. They often demand all kinds of information, particularly if you resist this tactic: the formula of the product, the cost components, your firm's internal productivity and so on. Some types of buyer, particularly the calculators (see Chapter 7) build complex cost models to bolster their argument. If they get information from several suppliers these models could be reasonably accurate, and over time they will get more so.

This is where the buyer says 'According to my model, it's clear that you need to offer me a lower price. I can see the crude oil price makes up about 20 per cent of the cost of your product, and it's fallen by 10 per cent since our last negotiations, so I want to see that reflected in your quote.' It's tempting to respond 'You're right, obviously, that the oil price has dropped, but that makes far less difference to our internal costs than you're estimating.' The buyer might agree to amend the model if you can back up your argument, but you're locked now into an assumption that cost-plus is the correct basis to quote on, and that changes in external prices that the buyer can monitor must be reflected exactly in your own pricing.

Clearly this tactic is focused on getting concessions, either now or in the future.

Diminished value stories

Salespeople have a tendency to market their product as different from, or better than, the competition. They will point out the benefits of their product, such as lower running costs or added functionality. This tactic is used by sellers to try to sell a value story and move away from buyers' cost-plus thinking. Buyers, however, especially if they are working from a cost evaluation plus margin, see the development costs of a product basically as sunk costs. 'It's already spent,' they argue, 'and that won't change whether you sell me this product or not.'

Buyers could potentially counter value selling in two ways: by dissociating the offer from the price, or by preventing value selling. Using the first these tactics, *disassociating the offer from the price*, the buyer lets the salesperson explain some of the benefits, but then counters by mentioning benefits that other suppliers offer. If the salesperson gets them to agree that some of the benefits or functionality are unique to their product, the buyers claims these are not relevant and don't add value to the company.

Buyers using this tactic say, for example, 'We've given you the specifications we require and your product seems to meet them. So do the other suppliers who have quoted to us. We recognize some of the benefits you describe, but we don't have a major preference between the contenders in terms of functionality. What does worry me is that your quote is on the high side.'

The second tactic, *preventing value selling*, will be taken care of either in the meeting set-up, where the buyer chooses not to be supported by technical staff and claims not to understand the technical differences, or by a clear message that the buyer does not want the salespeople to have off-line discussions with other functions during the negotiations. During tender processes in particular there tends to be a strict protocol for sharing information, which makes value selling difficult or even impossible. Clearly this way of managing value selling is more linked to power balance, and tends to work better if the sales side have few direct contacts in the customer organization.

'Diminished value stories' is a tactic that focuses on pushing for a concession.

Changing the negotiation team

A proven tactic to change the dynamics of the discussions is to change the negotiation team halfway through the discussions. This change could be done on either the buying side or the selling side. If done on the buying side, the selling side is just confronted with a new face. When it is done on the selling side, it also tends to mean that more communication is required upfront. Alternatively the buying side could request a change on the selling side. One way to do this is to request that a more senior person attend the meeting.

One benefit of changing the team on both sides is that pre-locked-in, or 'almost' agreed, points can be taken as a new starting position for the discussion. It can also be a delaying tactic – 'Sorry, but I'm new, and we need to look at the whole thing from the start' – or a way of applying increased pressure: 'We've taken Mary off the team because it's clear she wasn't making progress in achieving our goals', 'I know the previous buyer was pretty close to you. I'm more open to bringing in new players.'

A buyer's request for a change on the selling side is also a way to increase pressure. In general terms, too, more senior salespeople are prepared to take bigger risks and to bridge wider gaps than they would allow their account managers to do. Also they tend to have less background knowledge of the account (on issues such as growth opportunity and negotiating style), so they tend to see bringing in the sale as the only focus. The pressure on the senior person is higher too, as it would undermine their position in their own company to lose the account.

'Changing the negotiation team' is a tactic that has two effects: it adds confusion, and in that confusion there is a chance that the power balance will change to the benefit of the buyer.

Bringing in a new supplier or new item

Most salespeople know their competitors well, and therefore when they carry out Porter's five-forces analysis, they tend to know where they stand. The pitfall is that they only seem to look at known competitors, not at potential new entries or alternative products. Therefore a known tactic to change the power balance is to bring in a new player, explain that the buying company is willing to develop this new source, even perhaps investing with them to change the supply landscape. In most cases the starting point is that the new supplier will not be 'like for like' with the incumbent. Nevertheless the new position could be used as leverage, even if the new source is not capable of meeting all of the requirements.

Working on removing the need for an item entirely is also a great strategy, and brings in a level of new competition.

A supplier mined a special product, and owing to its quality only the one mine served an entire industry. The supplier was bought by a private equity firm that read the unique situation and overnight increased the prices by 60 per cent, and all customers had to accept the increases, making the business very profitable. Two years later the volume of sales suddenly started to drop dramatically. A few key players in the industry had worked on alternatives and changed away from the product as far as possible. The new owners had been warned of this, but had believed no other supplier could offer the same material. They were right on that, but they forgot that this gave an entire industry a strong reason to reformulate the products and avoid using this single-sourced material, which was in any case certain to run out at some stage.

Existing suppliers should not take it for granted that alternatives will not do the job, but work on tactics to fight for their customers (unless they have consciously decided they are prepared to lose some of them).

This tactic is aimed at creating a different power balance in a standard Porter way by bringing in an alternative product or by bringing in an alternative supplier.

Supplier listings

When companies start improving their purchasing processes, they tend to have a wide range of suppliers, often with new suppliers coming in regularly. Obviously one of the first actions is to rationalize the supplier base. Additionally, as companies grow by acquisition, this too prompts them to reduce the number of active suppliers or to change the position that active suppliers have (see the section in Chapter 8 on supplier portfolio management).

In order to build leverage from a supplier reduction programme, buyers start a process of cross-functional supplier tendering. In return for being put on (or staying on) the approved supplier list (its name varies), existing suppliers are normally asked for their best offers on *existing* business as well as concessions on their future business. If their offer is satisfactory they will be allowed to continue business in the future, and are likely to gain business as other suppliers lose their listing. Supplier listings are a very common process.

'Supplier listings' is a tactic that pushes for concessions.

A good example of a supplier listing programme is a US-based food company that introduced a 'gold-level status' for its suppliers in a supplier rationalization process. Suppliers were told that unless they made this gold-level listing, they would no longer be briefed on new products. They were expected to 'invest' in their gold-level status by offering price reductions on their current portfolio, joint development resources, stock-holding arrangements and other supply chain benefits. In return they were allowed to compete for the business of suppliers that did not qualify (by matching their terms) and would receive all new briefings (but no guarantee of winning contracts, of course). This process brought the customer significant immediate savings, so it was not a major surprise to see a re-run of the process two years later, when the company offered suppliers the opportunity to qualify for 'platinum-level status' with similar benefits. What basically happened that a certain 'status quo' was maintained, the tail-end raw materials were moved to all the key original players and the development opportunity for the key players was actually unchanged. It will be interesting to see what name they give to the next round of upgrades.

In reality all the company's major suppliers felt obliged to meet the terms and they all qualified. So they continued to be briefed but there was no large volume of business to be picked up from suppliers who opted out, because only tail-end volumes were on offer. This was not enough to justify the suppliers' investment in the process.

Buyers and negotiation tricks in pricing discussions

There are many smaller tricks that are also used in good price negotiations. We could fill a book with them and still have people mention additional ones. This section introduces some key ones that buyers tend to use and the counters that sales professionals could give. The examples are around price concessions, but similar tricks are used with different term discussions.

Denial

Most sales professionals sometimes resort to 'putting a gun against the head of the buyer to get them to agree'. Buyers can respond by ignoring the message completely. So for example, the salesperson says 'We really need to increase our prices, as our input costs have gone up quite significantly. Take a look at these market reports and you'll see what I mean.' The buyer's reply: 'I propose a 5 per cent reduction in pricing for the next quarter.'

Delay

We have already discussed how games with time are very important. A few tricks buyers can use for this are listed below.

Rescheduling/no availability

The purchasing manager's assistant calls you the day before the meeting and apologizes on behalf of the buyer: 'Unfortunately they can't make the meeting and it will have to be rescheduled. The buyer's diary is very full, but she could fit in a meeting in four weeks' time.'

Move decisions to others

A buyer says 'I personally don't agree with this concession, but it's not my decision anyway. This needs to go to my manager. I'll get back to you in a few weeks.'

Request for more information

There are two reasons for employing this tactic: to better understand the proposal or just to delay the implementation. In the first case, the buyer wants the information so as to find new opportunities to negotiate (now or in the future) on aspects of the terms. Sales professionals need to judge carefully what information to give out and what requests to refuse.

In the second case, a buyer says something like 'While I understand your rationale for this proposal, I'd like to see a joint team working through all the ins and outs. We need to seek opportunities to mitigate the impact through joint cost-reduction initiatives. While that's happening we'll have to keep things as they are.' This can be hard to fight, as the request looks so sensible, but the delay will save the buying organization money, and cost the seller.

Push it up the organization

This tactic has several effects. First of all it delays whatever is going to be implemented (what sales professional dares to implement a change while people are still talking?). Secondly it is a known effect that people higher in the organization tend to make concessions they would fire the people reporting to them for. A buyer says 'I want to see your boss. He should tell me this to my face and not stay in the "safe zone" and send you as a messenger', or 'I want your boss to meet mine.'

The best sales reaction is to arrange the meeting. There's also a question of whether the changed terms should be applied until the meeting takes place.

Play a personal card

There are many ways of doing this effectively, and particularly if the sales-person and the buyer have a good relationship, this tactic will work very well. Sometimes the player produces an extreme emotional reaction, either real or acted up.

To generate sympathy, they protest 'You can't do this to an old friend like me', or 'I thought we had a good relationship and now you come up with this', or 'I know you so well that I'm sure you personally don't agree with this. So how can we work this out?' Alternatively to build tension, they say things like 'This is exactly how I always viewed you and your company's behaviour', or 'Get out of my office! I'm putting you on the blacklist. I don't ever want to see you here again.'

The sales reaction to this kind of overwrought emotional reaction is difficult. The best way forward is a sympathetic approach. 'If I could have avoided it I would, but given the situation I don't have any alternatives.' When anger erupts, the best way is to let the emotion get out, ensure that the other party calms down, then let them save face ('I understand your feelings', even if you think it was over the top or faked for effect). Then leave, and contact the person a few days later to discuss a follow-up.

Using (semi) business reasons

Buyers could use business reasons (real or invented) to counter proposals. This is often combined with other tactics. So they say 'We can't pass this on to our customers, so you're asking me to take a direct hit on my bottom line', or 'I need time to implement this, so could we phase it in?' or 'In our relationship I expect you to take part of the hit. We are in this together through the good and the bad times.' Superficially at least, all these are rational responses, and they call for a measured reply. It's best if you have anticipated them so that you have an answer ready to give.

Power play

Depending on the power balance, buyers might be in a very strong position and decide to play it hard. Alternatively they might play it hard when their position is not that strong, just to test the waters. Typical responses are 'You are the only one coming with such a request', 'The answer is NO', 'So what are you going to do, not supply me? You've just give me an excellent reason to start on my supplier rationalization programme', or 'First sort out the problems we've had with you as a supplier before you even consider coming to us with proposals like this.'

The challenge here is that many negotiators go into a discussion without preparing their 'walk-away point'. How many sales professionals get the instruction, 'Push through this change/increase but don't lose the customer'? While that is a very understandable desire, what do you expect the sales professional to do? Actually if you implement changes without ever losing a customer, you have probably not pushed it to the point where you get the value you are paid to create.

The power of summary

In this tactic buyers summarize the agreement, snappily and slightly bending what was actually agreed to their own advantage. They are betting that the sellers, even if they recognize the subtle change, will let it pass rather than make a fuss. This is a great tactic for checking how hard a position is. If the seller picks up on the change and protests, the buyer can always apologize for not fully understanding the proposal, or protest that this was just a quick summary, leaving out some of the nuances.

It is important for salespeople to understand all these operational tactics and many more. If you see through the tactic, understand how to counter it, and keep in mind your own strategy and the direction of the customer portfolio; that will enable you to deal with any of the tactics used by buyers.

The seller's response...

This chapter is so full of helpful tips for the seller that there is little left to add, so I will raise just one issue: psychology.

If you think the buyer has all the power, then you are probably right. Think about that. We can very easily talk ourselves into a position of weakness and vulnerability, and for a variety of reasons.

Most likely, we think less of our own position when we fail to prepare, and most particularly when we fail to prepare by giving consideration to the customer's position. When we view the world from the buyer's perspective we also see their vulnerabilities and understand their fears. This is not to say that we should exploit them, rather that we reassess the balance of power, and so give ourselves more confidence. It is to be hoped that reading this chapter has gone a long way to curing us of the sin of one-sided preparation.

The next most likely cause of low confidence when entering the negotiation is the pressure applied on the sales professional by their own side – anxious sales managers, nervous sales directors. For any such reading this, remember that your own role in the negotiation process is to build, not undermine, the confidence of your front-line people. Sending them in to 'no option' or 'no alternative' negotiations is unlikely to build their confidence – a demand that they should achieve a 10 per cent price increase across all customers without losing any is such a circumstance.

Another reason is the realization that buyers probably do this kind of thing more often – they may be having the same negotiation with six suppliers, and we all know that practice makes perfect. Remember the cliché about negotiation: negotiation is a process where money and experience come together; the people with the experience get the money, the people with the money get the experience. So, what to do about it? Try to practise the negotiation in advance, perhaps with your boss (which may just help address the preceding point), or even better, with your own purchasing professionals. At the very least, rehearse it in your own head by imagining the least pleasant comments or toughest questions and preparing your response.

Finally, and in many ways most damagingly, we do ourselves down because we see no alternative to success, as laid down in our bosses' instructions. As a part of your preparation, write down (and I mean *write* down – the written word is often a great reducer and softener of imagined worries) your BATNA. This is your Best Alternative To a Negotiated Agreement – in other words, what will result if we don't come to the handshake across the table?

The BATNA gives you your fallback position, always very valuable in the psychology of negotiation. If you feel all your bridges are burned, you may do something foolish. If you realize that 'failure' to agree isn't so bad after all, because the written word of your BATNA shows you so, then you are more likely to be resilient and rational in the heat of the moment.

The BATNA is not a licence to be complacent; it is a mechanism for promoting good sense. My best advice is to try it the next time you are preparing for a negotiation; you will soon appreciate its value.

10 Price management: managing the buyer

A burning question for a lot of salespeople is whether and how buyers will accept price increases. The buyer who gets enthusiastic when presented with a proposal for a major increase probably doesn't exist, any more than there is a sales professional who gets a kick out of making less margin, but it *is* possible to maintain or even improve the relationship while increasing the price. The key for success is *knowing how* to do this.

This chapter explains some key fundamentals that will allow sales professionals to work the price agenda, while causing little or no damage to the buyer relationship.

There are four key elements in managing the presentation of a price increase to a buyer:

- the previous pricing relationship;
- timing;
- communication;
- process and follow-up.

If all of these points are managed well, there could follow a good healthy discussion on pricing. You must expect the discussion to be challenging, with a lot of pushing back and arguments up and down. While the objectives of the buying and the sales side are not aligned (both want to maintain margin, but for different companies), having a good process between the parties will help to advance both their objectives.

This book does not try to detail all the background and principles of setting and managing prices, or to discuss in detail effective communication and building a world-class process. All of these subjects are large enough for a book in themselves. The focus here is on how buyers look at the different pricing mechanisms, and how the buyer can be influenced or managed from the sales side to allow price increases.

The previous pricing relationship

Managing price consistently is crucial for successful margin protection. In general there are two ways to set prices; value pricing or cost-plus pricing.

With *value pricing* prices are set to reflect the value that the item creates for the customer. The value creation is assumed from the sales side, and in principle should be independent of the costs of making the item. Unfortunately it is not easy to gauge the value of an item for a *specific* application and *specific* customer, and not infrequently the real value is higher or lower than that assumed by the supplier. Having a real value proposition for a specific customer or industry segment requires quite an insight into the customer's processes and products. This insight will normally not come from a simple operational or tactical relationship, such as the standard buyer–seller interface. It is more likely for value opportunities to be understood when companies have an increased level of working together, for example when they are moving towards key account management processes. The largest pitfall is to assume that value is constant across an industry (without understanding the details of each of the industrial players), as what could provide significant value for one player in the industry might deliver hardly any value for another.

A remark that buyers hear frequently is 'We don't understand why you don't see the value of our products. Your main competitor does!' Most buyers respond with a combination of a laugh and irritation. The irritation comes because this implies the buyer is an idiot. The laugh comes if the buying company has done a full analysis of the product and has concluded that it does not add much value to their process or products. It will serve the salesperson right if they are told 'In that case, I hope you make a lot of sales to my competitor.'

Value pricing is seen by a lot of salespeople as the way to move away from an ongoing price discussion with buyers. Perhaps that clarifies why there seems to be a natural tendency on the sales side to sell all kind of items based on a unrealistic value proposition (at least as it is presented in the selling process).

In the alternative model, *cost-plus pricing*, prices are based on the costs of making the product plus a margin. Normally that margin is determined based on competitive factors and industry standards, and it varies from sector to sector as a result. The margin could be even be negative at some periods (if market prices are below the cost price), but in the long run it will need to be positive.

Depending on the buyers' leverage, they will have an opinion on the appropriate level of margin (either as a percentage or as an absolute figure). They recognize the potential for the market to move margins down, but are less willing to accept that it can move margins up (typically commenting, for example, 'A 5 per cent margin is enough for these products').

It is crucial to manage items with cost-plus pricing well. A key element is a good level of transparency over cost movements, both up and down. There is an understandable tendency to hold on to a higher price while the underlying costs are dropping in order to create some additional margin, but this will create a level of distrust in the relationship. Competitive elements will immediately be triggered. Cost-plus pricing does not automatically mean an 'open book' relationship, but rather a generic level of understanding of the main cost drivers.

Most salespeople seem to believe that selling a value proposition will protect the margin better than selling at cost-plus. This might not actually be the case. First of all, in a value proposition the price is detached from the costs, while in the end the margin that a company makes on the item is still dependent on the cost of producing it. Hence if the costs start to increase significantly, the margin could take a significant hit. Repairing that margin challenge by moving into a cost/price discussion might have a number of effects:

- The value/costs equation might now be under serious challenge, unless the alternatives move the same way.
- The buyer might become more forceful in demanding both internal and external proof of the additional value created by this item, particularly when there exists a more commodity-type alternative.
- The buyer would not necessarily understand the key cost drivers for that item, and their interest on those cost drivers might actually be unhealthy for the long-term margin levels of the item.

As a consequence it might be difficult in the short term to repair cost-driven margin challenges on value-priced items. Another problem occurs when a competitor in the market chooses to price their alternative using cost-plus, which tends create a lower price than value-priced items. This regularly happens when companies start to source in so-called 'low-cost' countries, where they help new entrants to become major suppliers, with a margin level (and expectation of the supplier) that is significantly below that of existing suppliers. The existing suppliers tend collectively to react too late to the new situation, and in many cases it drives them out of the business.

An even bigger dilemma for salespeople occurs when they have managed the pricing as if they are selling a value item, not sharing cost data with the buyer, but in reality the item is cost-plus priced, with cost drivers that could fluctuate very significantly. The sales logic behind not sharing cost information is normally that to share it might lead to a detailed margin discussion with the buyer (and this fear is at least partly justified). However, modern buyers have so many tools available that for key items they are very capable of building (and will indeed have) detailed cost models. So the risk of sharing information is limited, because the buyer already has much of it. The key worry should be the fact that margins cannot be protected on cost-plus items unless you are prepared to discuss the cost drivers. Again this does not necessarily mean going into open-book costing, but it does mean ensuring that the buyer understands some of the volatility of the main cost drivers. Hiding costs does not leave too many options for a price increase based on a costs rationale.

The fact that buyers have a natural tendency to think in cost-plus terms could represent a real opportunity for salespeople who manage this smartly. Cost-plus thinking requires the buyer to form a view on the costs, and in some ways they have access to better industry-wide information than the individual salesperson. If you play a part in the creation of the cost model, you can certainly influence the drivers. And when you know how the buyer's cost model is constructed, you can influence the buyer's view of those cost drivers through constant communication, and hence be effective in preconditioning the buyer before negotiations.

To summarize the major pitfalls and opportunities:

- Don't assume value. Only go the value route if you can prove value for a specific customer.
- Don't believe your own marketing stories. If too many customers tell you that they don't see value in your offering, there probably is no value in it for them.
- Only go for value pricing if the margin delivered is significantly higher than you could achieve by using a cost-plus process, so that cost movements do not immediately tempt you to leave the value-pricing model and revert back to cost arguments.
- Understand that buyers think in cost-plus terms. Therefore, with costing based on value pricing the pressure does not go away.
- From a buyer's point of view, if discussions move from value to cost-plus, from that moment onwards the pricing discussions are cost-based (though perhaps with a high starting margin).

Cost-plus pricing requires a lot of communication with buyers to ensure they understand the key cost drivers. That communication could also be used effectively for preconditioning.

Timing of pricing discussions

There is usually plenty of choice here, but timing is everything. Yet it is strange that most companies have this timing aspect completely wrong.

There are two key elements in timing price discussions. First, what are the customer's key milestones for setting internal costs (at what intervals, perhaps quarterly or annually, and when)? And second, what are the timelines that other suppliers to this customer follow? This means not only the direct competitors for the similar items, but also all other suppliers as they compete with you over the buyer's total spend.

Understanding the customer's financial planning cycle, including the timing and content of the targets (price, costs and others), is a key to ensuring effective preconditioning of buyers.

In most cases suppliers seem to bring up pricing after an internal business review, where the conclusion was drawn that margins were not as high as they should be. As consequence the sales force is sent out to do a 'price drive'. Even if the communication from that point onwards is excellent and the process is well managed, the chance of success is limited as the timing is unlikely to be well chosen. Furthermore, it is unlikely that the subject has come up during previous meetings, so preconditioning has probably been weak.

Getting the timing wrong will have two main results. First, the buyer will be taken by surprise, causing a strong reaction. Budgets might be already set, including the buyer's bonus targets. Therefore the discussion tends to shift from a business discussion ('What will it cost the company?') to a personal discussion ('How much bonus will this cost me?'). Second, you need to know what other sellers have done. If they have already used the budget head-space, while your arguments are still very valid (perhaps even more valid than those from some suppliers who have pushed through an increase), the money is already spent, so you will have to push harder and might still not succeed in driving the increase through.

So what is the right timing? It needs to be aligned with the financial year and the customer's forecasting process. There are key points in the year when buyers need to give their views on the market. It is essential that before those milestones the suppliers ensure their messages are heard. What's more, the timing needs to be consistent.

In summary:

- Understand the timetable of the customer's pricing processes, including the:

– long-term plan;
– budget;
– quarterly updates.

- Understand the buyer's timelines on agreeing pricing with all their suppliers (including those who supply products that do not compete directly with yours). Try to be early in the cycle. This increases your change of success.

- Understand the buyer's bonus-setting process to avoid a business discussion becoming a personal discussion.

Pricing communication

Pricing communication needs to be a constant flow, but tailored to the timing, as described above. Based on a theoretical annual cycle, an effective communication plan to manage pricing could look like the one shown in Figure 10.1.

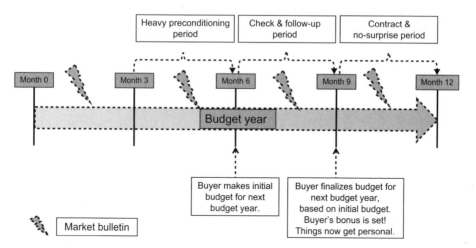

Figure 10.1 Influencing tactics: the annual buyers' timeline

In this cycle the buyer is constantly updated on cost developments, via every interface. The company also publishes a well-edited market bulletin that reviews major cost drivers that are not customer-specific, such as base materials and crop products, to influence the buyer's view of the main cost drivers. Owing to the well-aligned communication process, the buyer is well aware of what will most likely happen in price setting. Clearly this process only works when this information is shared consistently, is based on reality (but well edited to have the maximum effect), and is continued for a long period, both when costs are increased and when they are decreasing.

A second point concerns what to communicate:

- Only base data on key cost drivers? The question that immediately could be anticipated is: 'How do these affect my products?'
- Market data or actual costs? If there is a difference between the actual costs and the market (and your actual costs are higher), the likely response will be: 'We are not going to pay for your inefficiencies!'
- In market trends there is probably always a point when your company could have sourced its own materials at lower costs. The feedback is: 'Why didn't you buy your materials when the market was at the bottom?' If your firm has tried to anticipate price rises the market goes against it, the feedback will be around that.

The way you can handle these issues will depend on the type of customer and type of relationship. For your key and core customers, the communication will be different from that with your tail-end customers.

Pricing process and follow-up

From all that has been said above, it is clear that to manage prices well and consistently there needs to be a constant joint effort between marketing, product management and sales. The view has to be wider than the immediate competition, and communication, while partly generic, for maximum effect needs to be tailored to specific customers. You need to monitor what works in your market and what does not, and incorporate the feedback promptly into the process.

Companies tend to decide at regular intervals that price developments have not kept in line with cost developments. Sometimes this happens over years, particularly when companies have not been able to get price increases for a long period. However at some stage it becomes clear that the margins have been deteriorating so much that 'we have to do something'. Not infrequently this moment follows the annual review meetings where cost and margin developments are discussed. The management team then instructs the sales team to pursue a *price drive* focused on new contracts.

This 'ad hoc' process represents a major challenge. First of all there needs to be a range of internal discussions. Areas to discuss are:

- What increase do we need?
- How will customers respond to it?

- Do we have a general increase across the board or do we have specific increases by customer/item/category?
- What are the market dynamics?
- What is the risk of losing customers?
- What information should be shared with customers? How do we protect the higher margins on value items compared with cost-plus commodities?
- Do we commoditize the business?
- How do we prepare our sales force? Can they actually deliver the requirements (that is, do they have the skills)?

Recall the opening question in this chapter: 'Will buyers ever accept price increases?' Clearly the answer is yes, but it will only be possible without damage to the relationship if they are managed well, which means a well-controlled process, good communication and timing aligned to key customer processes. Before executing a pricing process it is advisable to understand where your items are placed in the Kraljic matrix, how the Porter five forces look for this item at this customer, and what the overall portfolio looks like.

The seller's response...

Buyers can be managed, and on price! They really do recognize value. These are joys to learn, but it is only true where great thought and carefully controlled behaviours exist on the supplier's side. There are some rules to be followed:

- Value is in the eye of the beholder.
- Value is only real if it impacts on a real and burning need.
- Value is only recognized if it is communicated effectively.

These rules can be best illustrated through a case study, picking up in fact on a case introduced in Chapter 8, the case of the 'procedure pack'. It will help to retell it from the beginning.

Figure 10.2 illustrates a supply chain within a hospital, and the departments concerned with sourcing, managing and using surgical instruments.

Figure 10.2 The hospital 'supply chain'

A particular supplier of surgical instruments, in pursuit of competitive advantage in a market that has become focused on price, and where it is hard to argue any kind of 'value' to the buyers, is launching a new product – the 'procedure pack'. This new idea aims to do the customer's thinking for them, delivering a complete pack of all the items required for any particular operation, or 'procedure'. It has several advantages over the old method of selling instruments as individual items, and not least the question of safety at the point of use – there being no risk of the surgeons finding themselves without an important instrument at a vital moment.

The supplier presents it to the buyer, who rejects it. All the buyer sees are premium priced products, gathered together in a box instead of sold individually. It is clear to the supplier that their true value impacts 'beyond' the buyer in the chain, with those who physically move, or manage, or use, the instruments, but that they have found a blocking decision maker in the buyer.

This supplier is up to the challenge and sets about fully understanding the nature of the pack's value beyond the buyer, as shown in figure 10.3.

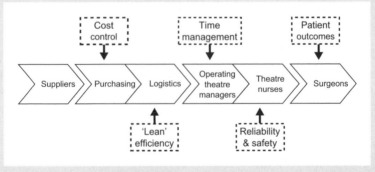

Figure 10.3 The nature of value in the supply chain

Now comes the choice: which value to pick? In theory, the intensity of the supplier's value increases as we move to the right-hand side of the chain – saving lives is 'more valuable' than smoothing the path of the logistics people. But this is 'in theory'. What if there have been no incidents 'in practice' suggesting any kind of problem with the old method of sourcing? What does this theory mean in any case to a buyer who is expected to save money from a shrinking budget and who is focused on financial measures of performance?

The supplier chooses to focus on the value brought to the operating theatre manager – the procedure pack saves them time, often as much as 40 minutes per operation. Now time can be turned into money, and so a value proposition can be put to the buyer, and in the buyer's own language.

Now comes a finesse. A better approach than the seller simply communicating this value to the buyer is to have the theatre manager do the communicating. Someone from the supplier's organization must take on the task of providing theatre managers with the ammunition to argue the case on the supplier's behalf.

So, the value has been considered in the eye of each beholder, it can be shown to impact on a real and burning need, and it is communicated to the decision maker by the most effective means. In such a case the buyer, unless blind or foolish, is almost compelled to recognize the value, and take a value-based approach to the price negotiation.

One last point to make on managing the buyer with regard to price. If forced to reduce your price, and there really is no alternative, agree with the buyer to do it in measured reductions over a period of time – two reductions of 2 per cent at six-month intervals rather than one reduction of 4 per cent. Not only does this hurt you less, but the buyer can be shown to have won twice – negotiating two reductions in quick succession. Timing is everything when negotiating price, whether it be upwards or downwards.

11 The purchasing agenda

Owing to the increased attention given to buying processes, the purchasing agenda has increased significantly over the last 10 years with all kinds of new subjects, directions, hypes, focus areas and so on. The scope of purchasing is by nature quite cross-functional, and today's supplier management processes touch all aspects of the buyer's company and major parts of the supplying company.

For sales professionals these agenda extensions offer both opportunities and risks, but the key is to recognize them and proactively decide whether or not to engage in the subject. In each of the next few sections there is a short description of the purchasing subject and how sales professionals can recognize when the customer is focusing on that area. The sections also discuss the opportunities and risks.

The most important items on the purchasing agenda (this list does not pretend to be complete) are:

- **Linked to supply chain/operations/logistics:**
  - in- and outsourcing;
  - inbound supply chain management, supplier networks, leanness and agility;
  - quality management (including vendor rating).
- **Linked to HR:**
  - sourcing of HR services;
  - code of conduct for buyers.
- **Linked to finance/legal/HR:**
  - risk management;
  - working capital management;
  - legal frameworks;

- financial reporting – focus on KPIs (leading/lagging, internal and external).
- **Linked to R&D/development:**
  - early supplier involvement;
  - innovation sourcing;
  - development outsourcing.
- **Linked to consumer/customer sales:**
  - market reports/purchasing marketing;
  - customer interfacing, customer joint purchasing efforts;
  - sustainability, social responsibility.
- **Linked to purchasing tools:**
  - e-sourcing (including e-bidding, reverse auctions and the entire e-suite of applications);
  - vendor management;
  - low-cost sourcing;
  - direct and indirect materials/services purchasing;
  - category management.

Supply chain-related purchasing activities

There is no doubt that the development of supply chain thinking has already had significant effects on the purchasing agenda, and this is likely to continue to increase in the future. This presents major risks and opportunities for suppliers.

Item availability and quality (total quality management) are key to ensuring ongoing business. The costs of 'non-performance', for example late or defective deliveries, are getting increasingly high. Lean and agile supply chains are more and more necessary because of fast-changing markets as well as the drive to tighten cash flow by having lower inbound stock levels. As a consequence there is an ongoing drive for inbound supply chain improvements.

To increase the effectiveness of the inbound chain there needs to be a better and wider discussion between buyers, the supply chain and salespeople focusing on lead times, batch sizes, batch cycle times and stockholding arrangements (such as vendor-managed inventory).

Another key item is 'time to market', the time required to go from an idea to a new item available for sale. In general the time allowed for this is shrinking as a result of competitor pressure.

The additional requirements are a balancing act between all elements of sourcing. For example low-cost sourcing could cause some tension over replenishment lead times and inbound stock situations. On the other hand, it might also not be optimal to have suppliers close to hand with a zero lead time but much higher price levels. The key is to value stockholding, lead times, responsiveness and prices against to each other to avoid an unbalanced situation.

More modern buyers are well aware of lean and agile supply chain principles, and will ensure their internal supply chain professionals are part of the sourcing decisions and supplier selections.

In general sales professionals (like buyers) are not experts in supply chain issues. If buyers start having discussions on this subject, it might be good to suggest that the experts from both sides meet up and discuss optimization opportunities between the companies.

The next sections offer a high-level overview of the main supply chain purchasing activities.

In- and outsourcing and offshoring

Companies used to be fully self-sufficient, with their own cleaning and catering services, their own tool shops, their own IT departments and so on. This self-sufficiency was followed by the first waves of outsourcing, when companies understood that they could not be expert in everything. It started in most cases with relatively 'safe' areas like cleaning and catering, and was followed by some more serious outsourcing efforts on maintenance and IT, and now it could now include even the full manufacturing or design processes. These changes have significant effects on the inbound chain, as primary items are suddenly not required directly any more by the buying company, but are required by a outsourced supplier or toll manufacturer.

In- and outsourcing offer risks and opportunities to the sales side. Outsourcing results in a reduced direct relationship with the end buyer, as outsourcing partners and toll manufacturers intervene. Not infrequently, these intermediaries also start to make some sourcing decisions on behalf of the ultimate end buyer. This creates opportunities and threats for sellers.

Sometimes there is an opportunity to change from being a supplier of parts to becoming the supplier of the entire final product or a major assembly. This forward integration might be an excellent opportunity for the supplier to increase the level of cooperation with the customer, and might widen the potential scope of supply to the entire market. A decision of this nature does, however, need to fit in the strategic direction of the company, and will be taken at a level outside the sales–buying interface.

Inbound supply chain management

Inbound supply chain management or operational purchasing has gained a lot of attention. In the past, getting hold of supplies ('never let production stop') was the key message; now the message is quite a lot more complicated.

With the increased focus on working capital (specifically, on a reduction of working capital to create more cash flow), fast-changing markets, longer inbound networks (as products tend to get slightly more complex and suppliers are regularly farther away), shorter product life cycles and so on, the level of challenge for the inbound chain has increased.

The new inbound chain needs to be lean (with limited waste in any form, and tight timing, lead times, stocks and so on) and agile (fast in adapting to changes required by end markets). Sometimes this runs counter to the trends to offshoring and low-cost sourcing activities. However, with early and cross-functional involvement of the supply chain, inbound supply networks could be set up that combine the benefits of low-cost sourcing with leanness and agility.

A good example of how low-cost chains and lean and agile chains are combined comes from the fashion industry. For the European market the first new designs could well have a relatively high-cost source such as Italy. These first shipments are intended mainly to test the market, and if there is a positive response, in parallel larger orders are placed in Turkey (with a mid-cost supplier) and Asia (with a low-cost supplier). The Turkish supply is available faster and will bridge the gap between the original Italian-made designs and the mainstream volumes from Asia. At the end of the season small top-up volumes could be ordered from Turkey or even from Italy to avoid either running out of stock or having major unsold stocks left. The value offer here came from a company that could offer this triple sourcing, instead of the buyer having to go to three different suppliers, and handle all the challenges of ensuring alignment on supply and quality. The price was competitive, though not as low as sourcing all deliveries from just the Far East, but value was also provided by taking away the risks for the customer.

The key question here for the sales professional is 'What is the service differentiation that I can offer to the customer?' In a total cost analysis, different service offerings have different values for the customer. Do you understand the value for each customer in the context of their inbound chain? If so, how can you make a proposal that increases the value for the customer as well as for your own company? The challenge is to recognize the hidden requirement for a different service. You could hear remarks like 'Your lead time is too long', 'We need smaller batch sizes as we have too much obsolete or slow-moving material', or 'We would like to seek opportunities for consignment stock.' These are descriptions of the consequences, and therefore they need to be investigated by experts to see what the real underlying issue (and therefore value opportunity) is.

Quality management: vendor rating

If there is no recording system in place, each supplier is as good as their last delivery: 'That is a really bad supplier. Take last week: the delivery was two days late.' This is frustrating for both the supplier and the buyer. But the real question is, was it the first late delivery in 10 years, or does it happen all the time? To judge suppliers purely on an 'incident log' is meaningless as it does not drive ongoing improvements.

To improve a process it is vital to start measuring the performance. Many companies now rate their suppliers on their performance. They share the results over past periods with to the supply base and agree forward targets.

The key criteria focus around the subjects mentioned in the section on supplier selection in Chapter 8, and include:

- Objective criteria:
  - delivery performance (on time in full, including documentation if required);
  - invoice performance (invoice errors);
  - quality performance (defect levels);
  - other leading or lagging indicators that could be measured numerically, such as lead times and cycle times.
- Subjective criteria (some of these could be measured objectively; most companies, however, treat them as subjective input), including:
  - service and responsiveness;
  - culture;
  - people;
  - innovation.

The aim in measuring these performance criteria is to have a continuous improvement drive between the buyer and the seller in the day-to-day business.

While most people working in supply chains understand the importance of measuring the performance of their suppliers, a lot of companies still struggle with doing vendor rating. The available support from most enterprise resource planning (ERP) systems tends to be weak, and most companies therefore design and implement specific solutions to capture both objective ERP-driven data (such as delivery/quality and invoice performance) and subjective elements such as people and innovation. The process for sharing information with the suppliers, to maximize the learning, also tends to be somewhat underdeveloped.

On the sales side it is crucial to understand how the customer sees you as a supplier. Frequently the view is based on feedback from the buyer or other key interfaces. Unfortunately these remarks might very well be biased at some times (aimed at commercial concessions). If the customer does not provide (and perhaps is not able to provide) data to your organization, it might be a good idea to supply the customer with measured service data on each interface from your own organization (if available), such as 'on time in full', and key quality data. To avoid quality or service issues becoming part of the power game of the buyer, it is advisable proactively to bring up any problems that happened in the previous period.

HR purchasing activities

In addition to the normal links that all functions have with their HR colleagues, the links between purchasing and HR increasingly focus on supporting the HR professionals in their sourcing activities. This does not mean the direct sourcing of human capital (that is, recruitment), but sourcing services to assist with this, and also sourcing of training, consultancy activities and payroll services.

Another important link for purchasing is the code of conduct, which is managed either through the HR or the legal or internal audit department. Many salespeople see differences between their clients in approaches to many aspects of the seller–buyer relationship, including (but not limited to) accepting gifts, guidelines around payment for trips, dinners, entertainment and hotels, different integrity standards and differences in safety, health and environment standards. Below some of the generic issues for buyers are discussed.

Code of conduct

Larger companies often have their key employees sign a generic code of conduct. Given the risk related to buying, in most cases buyers are (and should be) part of the key group for which the company lays down additional specific rules and guidelines.

The elements that are usually mentioned in the code of conduct or in the buyer-specific guidelines focus on:

- *Respect for the individual.* This cover subjects such as discrimination (on the basis of religion, race, gender, sexual orientation and so on), equal opportunities and freedom of religion.
- *Conflicts of interest.* Issues include making personal gains, conflicting activities (such as working for other companies, or having a major shareholding in other companies, especially suppliers and customers) and

or having family members as customers or suppliers. (Most of the time the rule states that if this is the case the employee should make it known.)

- *Confidential information.* Issues include using company information for personal gain (for example in a public company trading with privileged information), and sharing, consciously or unconsciously, information that could hurt the company in any way.
- *Bribery*, including topics such as the payment of bribes of any kind.
- *Community*, with the key focus on operating as a responsible citizen.
- *Safety, health and environmental issues*, with the key focus again on ensuring that the company operates as a responsible citizen.
- *Competition law.* This subject has gained a lot of attention in the last few years, and buyers tend to get detailed instructions on what, and specifically what not, to discuss with suppliers. Again this could be a subject where the selling–buying interface creates some challenges. Because buyers tend to have an increased understanding of the issues at stake, don't be surprised if a buyer stops you if you start to discuss your relationship with a competitor.
- *Gifts and entertainment.* This is a subject that is particularly relevant to sales professionals and buyers. Each company will have certain rules around accepting gifts. These could range from none to 'normal business practice'. While accepting cash is in most cases not allowed, it is understood that in many business relations in many cultures a small token of appreciation is traditional. Many companies that allow this set a maximum value.

The challenge is that these guidelines very significantly depending on the business environment and the local/cultural standards. Giving and accepting a gift is normal or even expected in some cultures, and not giving a token of appreciation could seriously damage the relationship or even worse be seen as an insult. The answer on questions around gifts is never as black and white as people simplistically put them in codes of conduct.

Some companies inform their suppliers that personal gifts cannot be not accepted, but if the supplier would like to show appreciation it is acceptable to make a donation to charity.

Finance/legal-related purchasing activities

The traditional relationship between the purchasing and finance functions centres on measuring and reporting results (in the past mainly with a particular focus on savings only). Reporting savings is still a key issue, and many companies still struggle with aligning purchasing results to the P&L account. Given the level of complexity and the detailed approach that this discussion would require, we will not go into detail on this; however it is an area where salespeople can help the buyers quite significantly with detailed cost reports.

In additional to that traditional relationship, in the last few years the agenda of finance has extended quite significantly, including areas such as risk management and financial reporting requirements (such as the US Sarbanes–Oxley regulations) and detailed contracting requirements under the US GAAP, IFRS regulations and so on.

The purchasing relationship with the legal function is focused on the contracting process, and in most cases around purchasing and sales conditions. Obviously the legal processes have become more important as the cost of getting them wrong has increased significantly. The types of relationship between customer and suppliers, which sometimes make them simultaneously competitors and customers, have become more challenging. The legal environment is changing fast, and when buyers and sellers are operating on a global basis the differences between countries are quite significant and could cause major problems.

Risk management

Many companies recognize that their risks do not stop with their own processes. In fact, with the increased buying levels of companies, including outsourcing of processes, most companies recognize that their main risk actually comes predominantly from their supply base. There are multiple examples where suppliers have caused major disruptions and significant damage further down the chain. The damage might be direct (such as a late delivery or quality issue), or indirect, in the form of reputational damage.

Professional purchasing organizations are expected to map their major risks and draw up action plans to handle them. Risks should be seen as any potential source of disruption, including:

- threats to security of supply (including single source, shortage of supply because of supplier allocations, crop failures and so on);
- lack of sustainability causing reputation damage;
- non-compliance in any form (with legal requirements, including labour laws, import regulations, material or service regulations and so on, and also quality non-compliances);
- financial issues (such as a supplier's financial stability).

Risk management for purchasing is still a relatively new area. Many purchasing organizations still struggle with this subject, and a lot of ad hoc solutions have been developed. Risks associated with purchasing should *not* be expressed in purchasing spend, but in terms of the effect on the bottom line of the buying company (in other words, as either sales or reputational damage).

Managing inbound supply risk starts with assessing the risk and the effect that a failed or reduced supply will have on the bottom line of the company. After the major risks have been analysed and ranked for effect, risk severity and frequency, a risk mitigation plan can be developed.

The Kraljic matrix is a good point to start the analysis because all items on the top right-hand side (high supply risk/high effect on the buyer's business) are the first priority. Items towards the right of the 'leverage' box are also important to assess, as are the items in the 'bottleneck' box that are growing quickly and have the potential to enter the strategic area. In Figure 11.1, items in the grey area require detailed risk analysis and action planning.

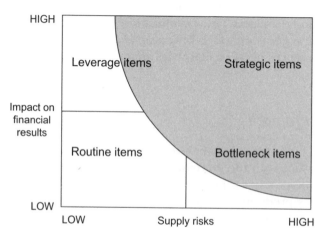

Figure 11.1 Risk management: using the Kraljic matrix to determine the key areas for attention

The make-up of the inbound supply chain is also quite important. An analysis of the critical bottlenecks in the chain might be required. Further detailed analysis would be required, for example, when an item is sourced from one supplier but could be produced in more than one factory, which actually reduces a number of risks. In contrast, even when there are multiple suppliers, the risk might be still quite high if all of these suppliers use a common supplier for their materials. The key risk here is one step backwards in the chain, where the bottleneck occurs. These risks are generally harder to analyse as it will require some deep supply chain knowledge and some excellent supplier relations to uncover this backward supply chain risk. And it is even harder to resolve it, as you need to start to build a business relation with a supplier you do not have a direct buying relationship with.

After analysing the risks and ranking them against the effect on the bottom line, a risk mitigation action plan should be developed. Elements that need to be part of that plan are:

- The analysis of the risk (severity, frequency and likelihood).
- Mitigation opportunities such as:
  - alternative sourcing opportunities;
  - alternative items;
  - reducing usage of the items;
  - additional safety stocks;
  - working with suppliers to limit sourcing risks, which could include long-term contracts to secure volumes, or supplier in-house back-up plans.

It is important for salespeople to pick up signals that the buyer is working on a risk mitigation plan for certain items. First of all this gives a good indication of where the buyer positions the item in the Kraljic portfolio. It also offers an opportunity to discuss relative margins and long-term contracting, and to move the discussion away from direct price pressure by offering a reduced risk scenario.

Working capital management

With the increased focus on cash flow and cash management, in most companies purchasing has worked to improve working capital by extending payment terms and moving stock down or away from the balance sheet by smart stock arrangements with suppliers. Moving stock to different points in the inbound chain will arguably not lead to cost reductions in a fully transparent chain. In theory, if prices are based on costs and the power of buyers and sellers is balanced, costs would only go down if total stocks are really reduced.

However, supply chains are not fully transparent and buyers' and sellers' positions are mostly not fully balanced. Suppliers and customers have different motivations to move into a stock arrangement or work on the working capital agenda:

- The arrangement could be pushed through by one of the parties, normally the buyer.
- The supplier could decide to offer better working capital arrangements as that could be a real differentiator from the competition (though potentially costly, depending on the cash situation of the company).
- The supplier could decide to offer better working capital arrangements because in its part of the world the cost of capital is relatively low. For

example for years Japan had zero or very low levels of interest, so payment terms of over 120 days were not unusual. This position could be leveraged by the buyer to seek increased payment terms with other suppliers.

- More complex stock arrangements, such as stockholding for the customer, even combined with investing in storage areas at the customer premises, will increase the level of cooperation with the customer and will reduce the chance of the buyer moving quickly (and in the face of low switching costs) to another source.
- A more complex stock arrangement is sometimes an underrated benefit for the sales side: it can be a major benefit, as it really locks in the customer. While there are costs associated with it, the costs of keeping the customer in a fully flexible situation (which means low switching costs) might be higher. The same is true of hunting for new customers rather than discounting prices to the existing customer base.
- Moving stock to a stock arrangement like vendor-managed inventory might also reduce the costs in the chain. However, this will only be the case if the vendor has a better capability to manage the stock, for example holding the same stock for more than one customer, hence reducing the aggregated safety stock.

The working capital agenda adds additional challenges and opportunities. While the payments terms extensions could be managed within the purchasing function, managing stocks smarter is a very cross-functional subject that requires purchasing to link to finance, supply chain and operations in quite some detail.

Legal frameworks

Clearly the world of contracting does not become easier. With risk mitigation processes hitting all companies and a requirement for increased performance by both items and supply chains, clearly the legal agenda is becoming more and more challenging. Major commitments need to be covered by detailed, carefully negotiated and complicated contracts to ensure that both parties know very well their responsibilities and their risks.

As a consequence buyers nowadays receive significant training on a wide range of legal aspects, such as:

- generic contract laws (including subjects like pre-contractual liabilities, and written and oral contracting);
- standard terms and conditions – the legal battle of forms between purchasing and sales conditions, including subjects such as liabilities, *force majeure*, guarantees, exclusivity and confidentiality;
- international trade laws;

- competition laws, mainly focused on US and European regulations;
- signing authorities (internal and external).

While all of these might seem very much 'administrative issues' and 'food for lawyers', understanding these subjects will give you a significant advantage in the discussion process. Modern buyers, while clearly not being legal experts, have enough knowledge to discuss the outlines of a contract, frequently better than the average salesperson. As a consequence they will have a better chance to agree issues to their advantage.

It is vital for salespeople to ensure they understand the principal legal requirements of their company and do not leave the discussion of this purely to the legal team, as this might frustrate the relationship (and certainly does so when commercial agreements made by sales are wiped out afterwards by the legal team).

Financial reporting

With the development of the purchasing function, its visibility and more importantly its results have enjoyed an increased level of interest. While the purchasing function emerged from an administrative background, most purchasing organizations have struggled (and some still struggle) with transforming their raw data into effective and useful information. Most ERP systems do help with getting to grips with the transactional data such as volumes, prices, suppliers and vendor ratings (the transactional facts), but generating useful information that could be used for financial reporting (linked to the P&L account) and even more importantly budgeting (including linkages to 'objective' market information) has proved to be more problematic.

Without going into detail, there are many ways to look at purchasing results. In principle it looks simple: the current price minus the previous price, multiplied by the current volume, should represent the price effect of an item. But it is important to take into account issues such as:

- volume, mix and currency effects;
- non-price savings (such as alternative items that provide significant savings in cost of use);
- savings versus market pricing (on true commodities);
- the time lag between invoice-based purchasing results and the effect on the P&L account.

Well-managed companies have moved to some sort of balanced scorecard, where as well as price effects (or purchasing results as they are frequently called) they also report on working capital management, sourcing activities, innovation activities, functional development and other focus areas. When implemented very well, this scorecard is linked directly to the objectives or 'critical success factors' of the company.

Understanding how the customer reports internally can help salespeople in better positioning their items, by enhancing the sales and marketing story in order to support the buyer's reporting methods. Not only will this build a more effective relationship, it will also enable better preconditioning of the buyer.

R&D/development-related purchasing activities

It is now widely accepted that the only effective way to manage costs consistently is to ensure that purchasing (as the representative of the suppliers) is involved early in the development cycle. While that principle is accepted, the execution still creates a number of challenges.

Innovation and sourcing new innovative products has also hit the purchasing agenda. Where in the past this was left to R&D, only moving to purchasing when new innovative items came into the mainstream, it has now become clear that purchasing needs to play an important part in ensuring innovation, through both existing and new sources.

Early supplier involvement

High on the agenda of purchasing professionals is early involvement in the development process for new products. Too frequently buyers are confronted with fully developed end products, with difficult-to-source items built into the design. Obviously these items automatically become an opportunity for future optimization, but would it not have been better if they were not used in the first place?

The early involvement of purchasing will ensure that the newly required items are investigated in a wider market context, and their sourceability (the availability, scaling opportunities and so on) is considered at the right point in the development process.

With purchasing processes moving more towards creating value, ensuring early involvement in the development process is crucial. 'Design for costs' and outsourcing innovation (partly or in full) are themes that have hit the purchasing agenda.

For suppliers, being involved early provides all kinds of opportunities. First of all they might be able to influence the solution that the customer selects so as to create a referent position for their own product. And if they understand the development better than competitors do, there is a significantly higher chance to make a proposal that fits the customer's requirements.

Innovation sourcing

Sourcing of innovations is a second major sourcing agenda next to the low-cost sourcing agenda. In different industries it means different things, but clearly there is a drive to have suppliers more closely linked to the innovation process. In certain industries, such as the automotive sector, this is already a fairly standard way of working, while in the food business, as in many other businesses, this path has yet to be entered by most players.

Innovation sourcing is quite different from generic sourcing processes. It requires buyers to be open to new elements coming from completely different markets, from new and sometimes small players, and it requires them to understand in quite some detail their own company's innovation focus. Quite uncomfortable as well is that most of the innovation items start as 'bottleneck' challenges in the Kraljic matrix.

The added value that purchasing can deliver in the search for new innovative items is the direct link with current supplier relationships and the ongoing purchasing focus. The search for new innovative items can be linked just as well to existing suppliers relationships as to new sources. A buyer who has some ideas of what the research function is looking for might have contacts, or might know suppliers that (potentially) have the capability to make the newly required items.

Salespeople need to recognize the customer's innovation requirements, and ensure that they link via the buyer to other people in the customer organization. This is a process that would strengthen the relationship.

Sales/consumer/customer-related purchasing activities

Buyers need to have a good link with their own sales team in their own company to ensure that future cost projections or supply chain elements are well understood on either side. In the buying companies, the sales functions (working in most cases through product management) need to protect margins by pricing items right, and to do this they need a good understanding of future raw material and service costs.

Increasingly customers request more direct interfaces between the selling and buying company than just the traditional buying–sales interface. These often includes a direct link between the buying company of the supplier and the buying department of the customer. Subjects discussed at that interface could include collaborative buying and major cost developments.

The increased focus on supply-chain-wide initiatives around sustainability also requires additional attention. This requires the purchasing group to better link with its own sales teams to ensure proper communication, as well as understanding what the customer base of the company is looking for.

For sales professionals this part of the purchasing agenda has two major opportunities. First, internally, are you as a sales professional benefiting enough from this intrinsic knowledge in your own purchasing department? Do they provide this information or not? And if not, why not? Do you use your own purchasing team as a sparring partner to assist you with difficult external buyer interfaces? And externally, the buyers of your customers need your input/support on the information they have to share in their own organization. This is a potential opportunity to build a stronger relationship.

Market reports: purchasing marketing

It is essential that people who set prices and/or communicate with customers about price levels are very well informed about developments in the company's own costs for purchased items. Sharing that market knowledge with product management and then, via the sales group, with customers' purchasing functions could build significant additional value, both in margin protection and in improving the perceived value that the customers have of the selling company. They will appreciate its giving market information to them. Effectively influencing customers' buyers with the right 'pre-edited' market reports, but also building the knowledge base of the company's own sales force, requires more and more focus. Clearly the drive towards more openness on pricing and cost levels demanded by the customer will require the purchasing and sales functions within a company to work significantly better together.

Most purchasing teams have now developed a comprehensive, regular market report for the key internal stakeholders, with market information on key items, key market developments and a cost outlook. These reports include objective third-party analyses of the market, with acceptable third-party indices of price developments, but tend also to give an insight into the company's specific situation. Different reports are normally produced for management levels (high-level, more focused on the actual internal situation) and for the sales teams (more detailed and with information more geared to objective third-party data).

For suppliers' salespeople to give input to these reports represents a significant opportunity to strengthen the relationship, and also brings an opportunity to 'precondition' the customer in certain directions.

Customer interfacing and collaborative purchasing

Buyers frequently ask salespeople to bring functional experts into the discussions. When purchase costs are very significant in the overall cost of the company's products, buyers increasingly ask salespeople to bring their own buyers in to discuss cost developments directly. Clearly for the supplier's buyer this requires additional effort, as a buying–selling role is not the same as a buying role.

Collaborative purchasing is also being investigated more frequently, certainly during times of inflation in raw material prices. In a number of cases this leads to mutual benefits and increases the customer intimacy from the sales side.

Sustainability and social responsibility

In the last few years the sustainability agenda has gained significant attention from the boards of most large companies. With most companies being far more than 50 per cent dependent on incoming materials and services, this has led to more detailed management of inbound processes in line with the company's sustainability policy.

Incidents with sustainability issues on the purchasing side have hit many companies, and reach the press quite frequently. Raw materials or end products made by toll manufacturers, predominantly from low-cost countries, have received a lot of attention from lobbying and campaigning organizations. Among the major issues are the use of child labour, unsafe production methods or production environments, general labour conditions and problems with waste disposal. Clearly this public attention has had a significant impact on sourcing requirements throughout the whole chain.

As a consequence most companies have started to add sustainability criteria to their supplier qualifications. This has resulted in a lot of questionnaires hitting the chain, as each player tries to get an understanding of the sustainability challenges of the inbound supply chain as a whole. For most companies this attention is driven by managing risks, and there is therefore a lot of attention to the processes and systems used by the suppliers to ensure their sustainability, such as compliance with UN guidelines or certification processes such as ISO 14000.

The sustainability debate is closely linked to wider debates on globalization and diversity. It is difficult to determine how to manage a source that a competitor is happily buying from when your company perceives sustainability questions.

The main questions that buyers are confronted with (and as a consequence, the issues for salespeople) are:

- If there is a cost difference, what extra cost am I prepared to pay for a sustainable source?
- If my competitor is buying from the same supplier and there is a competitive advantage to that source, how do we manage this in terms of end market competitiveness?
- What are the norms to use in judging sustainability, based on global diversity in thinking on this subject?
- Is cutting a supplier relationship the best way to improve the sustainability situation long term?
- In purchasing terms what is the value of image?
- Is sustainable sourcing solely a purchasing decision? How can the company put it on a wider agenda?

Purchasing tools-related activities

Linked to the functional developments, purchasing tools have gone through a significant development process. A lot of purchasing departments have developed not just ERP systems but specific purchasing tools to make their management, reporting and document flow significantly more effective and efficient.

We cannot list every possible purchasing system here, but the main tools that purchasing departments have implemented are:

- Comprehensive *spend and forecasting* tools, enabling the buyer to see quickly at a high and detailed level all transactions and forecasts broken down by supplier, material, category and business. Quantitative reporting data can be extracted from these tools, and frequently they are used by several other functions to help them understand not only the numbers, but also other aspects of the purchasing transactions.
- *Supplier relationship management (SRM) tools,* which are tools for buyers similar to the better-established customer relationship management (CRM). SRM is used for capturing all the interactions with suppliers, and also for managing communications, briefings, projects and other market-supplier specific elements. Vendor rating tools are frequently a part of the SRM functionality.
- *E-connectivity tools,* providing platforms for reverse auctions, auctions, catalogues and e-enabled transactional information links between buyer and seller.

- *Project management tools*, which enable cross-functional projects to attack direct and indirect costs in a cross-functional way.
- *Contract and legal management tools*, which are used for managing contracts (on top of the ERP functionality) and communication with suppliers and different units that run on different ERP platforms.
- *Strategy tools*, allowing the development of cross-functional strategies, including thorough market analysis, and short-, medium- and long-term cross-functional activities.

The combination of tools allows buyers to be more effective and efficient as they drive information insight, both internally and externally. This allows buyers to focus more on the strategy part of the function and the development of increased market insight, including alternative sourcing.

E-sourcing

E-sourcing is the name for a large number of activities and tools that use internet technologies to gain efficiency in the purchasing processes. Among the tools and activities under this heading are catalogues for non-product-related materials and services, e-connectivity for the purchase of direct materials (in which the ERP systems from the selling and buying companies exchange information), and electronic requests for information (RFI) and requests for quotations (RFQ). However, the area that has gained most attention has been e-auctions, reverse e-auctions and other negotiation-linked tools.

Different e-applications serve different needs. In this section the most important and relevant e-tools and activities are summarized.

E-catalogues are generally set up for non-product-related areas to ensure the end-user buys approved materials from an approved source in a pre-agreed process. They can be general catalogues from the supplier (with a specific price list for this customer) or specific catalogues for a customer (running on either the supplier's or the buyer's server) or a mix of the two. Generally they are accessible to either all end-users or designated people in the buying company. Payment could be through normal invoice processes, but it is also quite common to facilitate the use of credit cards or more specific P-cards (purchase credit cards specific for companies buying from e-catalogues, featuring additional spend and usage features). E-catalogues could be maintained by the seller or the buyer. A service industry has also developed that links buyers and sellers via catalogue portals.

E-RFIs/E-RFQs are electronic internet versions of the standard paper/mail processes for getting a price proposal from a supplier. These processes aim to gain efficiency in the process of information comparison and quotation comparison at the buyer's end. They ask questions and provide quotes in a predefined format that can be loaded into an automated comparison system.

The benefits of the process for the buyers are that they receive predefined information from all sellers. For the seller, if the process is run correctly, the benefit is that the information given to one of the parties is equally shared amongst all sellers, giving equal opportunities to all competitors. The disadvantage is that it is difficult to include other information regarding the items, so the opportunities for value selling are limited.

E-connectivity is the name for a group of tools that link different seller and buyer information systems. Data might be shared on, for example, stock levels, orders, payments or forecasting information.

E-auctions, hated and loved by different people, are tools that allow buyers and sellers to negotiate online for a certain contract, with visibility to all parties involved. E-auctions have acquired a fairly negative reputation from many salespeople as they have seen that this tool tends to drive prices down. For the same reason many buyers see this tool as excellent for certain categories of materials and services.

All of the e-tools have their own area of usage. If we take the Kraljic matrix as the basis of categorization, Figure 11.2 shows how e-tools fit into it.

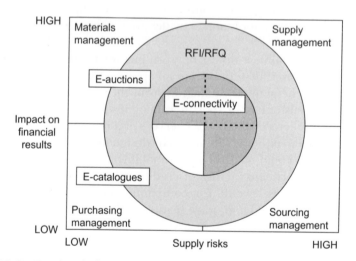

Figure 11.2   E-tools: which tools fit where in the different sourcing strategies
Source: adapted from the Kraljic matrix.

It should be noted that although in principle RFI/RFQ will work in all segments, it is probably less appropriate for bottleneck items because this is an area in which influencing techniques are quite important (certainly with new vendors).

Other elements will determine the fitness for purpose of certain e-auctions, including:

- The level of specifications. For example, how well do specifications really describe requirements? If it is difficult to be exhaustive about the requirements, the item will be less suitable for e-auctions.
- The industry competitiveness, which describes the degree of competitiveness in an industry, and often depends more on attitude than on the number of suppliers. If there is not a real competitive environment in a market, although there are multiple operators, it will be less suitable for e-auctioning.
- Risk and costs of switching suppliers. The higher the cost of change, the lower the fit with e-auctions.
- The relationship with existing suppliers. If a strategic relationship has developed and there is a significant common innovation or supply chain agenda, the area will be less suitable for e-auctions.
- The overall item mix with suppliers (moving to e-auctioning for commodity items might affect the relationship on more specialized items).
- Supplier qualification processes. For example, while switching to another supplier might be technically feasible, in certain industries it would create a requirement for re-testing of end products or customer approvals. The more difficult the supplier qualification process is, the less it makes sense to go into a wide e-auction (as that requires all suppliers to be pre-qualified).

A lot of salespeople see e-auctions as an 'evil' tool, mainly because of the major price reductions achieved when they were introduced. In reality e-auctions are not very different from ongoing discussions between buyers and sellers, but their introduction allowed buyers to generate competitiveness in situations where it had not been fully operative before. That caused a strong correction in some price levels. At first some sellers entered e-auctions with insufficient preparation, and committed to supply at price levels they would have never accepted if they had had the opportunity to think the process through.

However now that e-auctions are an established process, and are being used in a more balanced way, they actually offer salespeople an opportunity to reduce the sales workload on commodity items. It would be good if salespeople too started to see e-auctions as an additional effective and efficient tool with its own benefits. Companies that state 'we will never quote through e-auctions' really miss opportunities for good sales and they are probably more afraid of the unknown (or hurt by bad preparation in the past) rather than driven by economic logic.

Vendor management

Just as the sales side has seen the development of customer relationship management, the purchasing side has started to embark on supplier relation management. The key elements of SRM are:

- contacts;
- projects;
- relationship history, including meeting reports;
- vendor rating.

SRM has not yet reached full implementation for all buying teams, and there are some questions about how the administrative effort compares with the benefits.

Low-cost sourcing

In most companies there has been a significant effort to move production from traditional sources towards Latin America, Eastern Europe and Asia. This process started with basic raw materials and basic services years ago, but has now moved into the full sourcing of high-added-value materials as well. Certainly for this last category of low-cost sourcing, new suppliers had to be developed, a process that included quality and logistic processes.

For the buyers this opened new opportunities but also new challenges. Clearly the markets were in most cases unknown, trading cultures and habits were quite different, and new relationships had to be built and maintained. Low-cost sourcing has had both major successes and fatal failures. But the further globalization of the sourcing area has become a fact.

For traditional sourcing this meant a complete change in the costs and competitor reference bases. Traditional manufacturers and service providers have responded by making major changes in their set-up, either focusing on parts of the portfolio, partly outsourcing their products or changing their set-up to match the cost leadership level. In many cases it also changed the way customers work with agents and traders. While direct sourcing is now an option, agents and traders need to really add value in order to stay part of the supplier mix.

Traditional regional and local markets have in most cases opened up quite significantly to global competition, creating both risks and opportunities.

Direct and indirect materials/services buying

Generally companies have all processes related to direct materials and services reasonably well under control, including the sourcing and buying activities. More challenging are the indirect spend items and services, which could take up to 50 per cent of the total external spend. In many cases the financial and purchasing controls, and the systems to show the impact on P&L, are not necessarily well defined.

With the drive for ongoing improvement of results and the focus on on-going purchasing cost savings, many companies have moved into formalizing this area. Implementing (global) contracting groups, executing e-auctions, developing catalogues or start project 'cost teams' have had different degrees of success. This change was enabled by the emergence of e-tools for more efficient and effective handling of requisitions and purchasing transactions.

Category management

In organization terms, purchasing is developing more and more in the direction of category management, where a number of (lead) buyers are working in a (small) group on materials or services that have similarities. The most basic categories are defined around direct and indirect materials or services. These categories are normally then further split, for example natural materials and crops, chemicals and so on. Examples on the NPR side are MRO (maintenance repair and operating supplies) and site services (security, cleaning, catering, financial and legal services, and so on).

The benefits of category management is that materials in certain categories have similar attributes, and as a consequence working as a small group to source a category could avoid duplicated work and might deliver better cross-over of sourcing opportunities and ideas.

The seller's response...

There is a great deal to be mastered in this chapter, but the good news is that it is unlikely in any given situation that it will all be relevant. The key is to identify which of these issues are relevant to the buyer, and then make sure that they don't come as a surprise to you.

Buyers do not like to see your eyes glaze over (and they look for such things) when they raise a particular issue of burning importance to them. If 'risk management' is high on their agenda, then they will expect it to be high on yours, and will expect you to be up on what it involves.

This chapter will be helpful in keeping you 'up to speed' but you might take an even better course, and that is to bring in a genuine expert from your own organization. This is to make use of what we will call (in the next chapter) the 'cotton-reel' relationship, and it is a great way of indicating to the buyer that you recognize their concerns and mean to be of help. It even goes one better: it indicates that these issues are also important within your own company, and that is important in securing the customer's confidence.

12 Buying and selling relationships

Sales people like to talk about the relationship, sometimes in an almost mystical way as if this is the answer to all problems. Some buying organizations like to rotate the members of the buying team so that once a year the seller meets a new face, often as a deliberate way to handicap the development of 'a relationship'. Is this then an issue that divides sellers and buyers?

It's all about supplier positioning and the Kraljic matrix, described in Chapter 8 and illustrated in Figure 8.6.

Where a supplier is in the lower left quadrant, buyers will not want or expect a deep or complex relationship. Indeed, they prefer to have no relationship at all, buying through some automated method without the need for sales people.

In the top left box, buyers often prefer what sales people sometimes refer to as the 'bow-tie' relationship (see Figure 12.1).

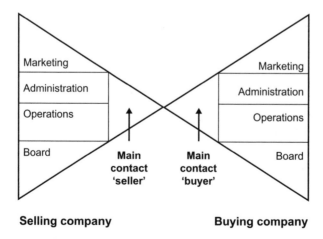

Figure 12.1 The 'bow-tie' relationship

The buyer needs someone to negotiate with, but doesn't want them getting too well informed – that might just give them ideas 'above their station'... Sellers don't like being restricted in this way of course – they speak of 'gate-keeper' buyers – but often it is for their own good (no, really!) If the deal is going to be completed on a simple price for volume basis then the buyer is saving them a lot of unrewarded effort in trying to 'penetrate the snail' (see Chapter 4).

If the supplier is positioned in either of the right-hand boxes – 'strategic' or 'bottleneck' – then there might be value to the buyer in allowing an expansion of contacts between the selling and the buying organizations. At its greatest extent, a relationship that sellers often call a 'diamond team' (see Figure 12.2) might be attractive to a buyer, if it were to result in greater security of supply, or speedier deliveries, better forecasting, improved quality, faster new product development, reduction of costs, or any other real and tangible benefit.

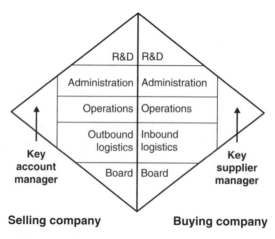

Figure 12.2 The 'diamond team' relationship

It would be a foolish buyer who denied such access, if genuine benefits result from it, but sellers should not regard this as a licence to 'roam the customer's corridors' in search of people to befriend and influence. Additional contacts of this nature can bring problems for the buyer, not least in the way that they can eat time – their own and their colleagues. It is in fact often a responsible buyer that protects their organization from over-zealous sellers anxious to build such diamond teams.

It is probably true that long-term relationships work to the seller's advantage, and in a situation where buyers want to keep suppliers 'sharp' and on their toes, they will perhaps act to disrupt relationships – the simplest method being to change the people involved. Ironically, one of the things that annoys

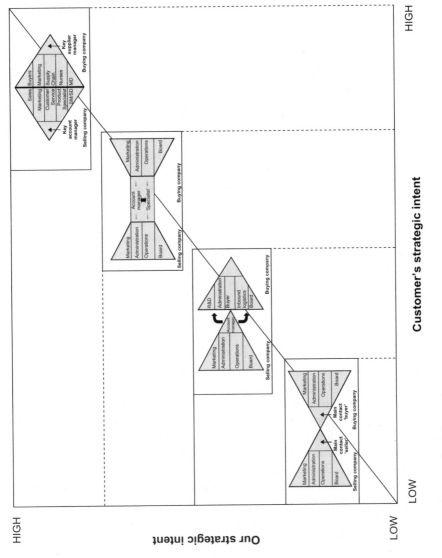

Figure 12.3 The relationship spectrum

buyers most is when a supplier does the same thing too often – the worst scenario being when they are clearly being used as a training ground for new sales representatives!

The key to finding the 'right relationship' is in the idea of mutuality (see Figure 12.3).

There are differing degrees of strategic intention for both seller and buyer in any business relationship, and the ideal outcome is almost always when there is a match: both sides need each other as much as each other. The buyer can, and will, manage the relationship – rationing it or developing it – in order to find that matching point. Bow-ties are most likely to be 'right' when strategic intentions are low on both sides. Diamond teams are 'right' when strategic intentions are high on both sides. There is a range of subtle steps in between, illustrated here by just two examples.

The next step to be 'allowed' the supplier, beyond the one-on-one relationship, may be where the seller has additional contacts beyond the buyer – what sellers might call the one-on-many relationship. Any buyers worth their salt will want to know who those contacts are, and why, and what benefit results to themselves as a result of those contacts. Without such questions, such relationships can easily get out of hand.

A more disciplined relationship may be what sellers often call the 'duet' or 'specialist' model, sometimes described as the 'cotton-reel'. Where buyers see the benefit of involving specialists from the supplier (meaning that they are there to help, not to sell), they will happily help pair them up with their own functional specialists. The key to success in such relationships is a clear agreement in advance of objectives and rewards.

So, who manages whom? Suppliers with diamond teams headed up by account managers, or key account managers often think that it is their job to manage the relationship, without stopping to think whether buyers wish to be so managed! Smart buyers might even encourage such illusion – particularly if it enables them to get a lot of free effort expended on their behalf. In truth, such relationships require high levels of trust on both sides, as well as clear rules and disciplines. Managed well, which almost certainly means managed from *both* sides, they can build significant value.

There is one final requirement that buyers will insist on if they are to entertain the notion of anything approaching a diamond team: the account manager must be able to demonstrate the ability to coordinate such a team, often cross-functional, and must have sufficient authority to make it work. Buyers will doubt the effectiveness of such ventures if headed up by new and junior sales people.

The seller's response...

Yes, long-term relationships work in the seller's favour, as do those relationships that encourage a breadth of contacts at all levels of seniority, and the involvement of multiple functions. So much so that sellers can sometimes be overeager to build their diamond team, treading on toes as they go. The 'bull in a china shop' account manager can cause a lot of damage in a short space of time through impatience and aggressive entry strategies, with the inevitable negative impact on trust and openness. The ultimate penalty paid for pushing too hard is a ban on additional contacts and an insistence that the seller provides one, and only one, point of contact for the buyer.

There are three rules to observe when building towards diamond teams:

- Get permission.
- Demonstrate the benefits to the buyer.
- Be a political entrepreneur.

The first rule is clear and simple – get the buyers' permission before forging contacts beyond them, and best of all, engage their help in getting the introductions.

Demonstrating the benefit is vital. Aim to communicate the positive results that will result from additional contacts, making clear how the customer, and the buyer, will benefit. Done well, such communications can help to enhance the buyers' status among their own colleagues, particularly if it can be shown to have been the buyers' good business sense and maturity of outlook that led to those introductions in the first place.

The third rule – be a political entrepreneur – requires a little more comment, perhaps best done through a case study.

A large multinational company wishes to have its suppliers move to electronic invoicing in order to reduce transaction costs. Most suppliers are keen to oblige but in some cases – the less sophisticated members of the supply base – there is a good deal of resistance.

Using their own political entrepreneurship the buyer targets the best of the reluctant suppliers and pressures them to respond more positively by saying that none of this supplier's competitors seem willing to help – a well-dangled carrot if ever there was one.

Let's now turn to the seller. The account manager wishes to oblige, realizing that this is a wonderful opportunity to gain competitive advantage, but is equally aware that there is a mountain of opposition within their own business – the operations function seems in denial that this is a genuine requirement.

So, in such cases account managers must proceed by careful steps, using their political entrepreneurship as they go:

1. They ask the customer if, in return for providing this new service, they can be introduced to other parts of the customer's business where they currently have no presence. Introductions only, no promises of business: they know that this is not a great deal to ask.
2. Once they see that this will in fact be possible they start to work on their own people: 'look what we can get in return.'
3. Over and above the immediate return, they point out that before long other customers will be making similar demands, and here is a wonderful opportunity to develop a new capability and be paid for it through new business.
4. Once the signs of internal support begin to show (and it may be necessary to involve senior management to press the issue and advance the case), the next step is to bring the functional experts together – the 'duet' described above.
5. By showing the customer that they are at least now ready to talk, they are better placed to secure those introductions to other parts of the customer's business.
6. The new introductions will present many new opportunities, and the political entrepreneur will aim to secure a quick win, in order to build the case to their own internal people that they are doing the right thing.

The happy ending is fourfold: the customer gets what they wanted, the seller wins some new business and has also secured a measure of competitive advantage, and the supplier has built a new capability ready to offer to other customers.

This is the political entrepreneur at work. Such entrepreneurs are people who know their way around the customer's organization and their own, and they have demonstrated three vital capabilities: vision, patience and the authority to make things happen. We should add a final requirement, and that is to make sure that the buyers see not only the benefit of what they have received but also the benefit of the extended relationship that got them there. This is true value management, and will help to keep the door open for the next time.

13 Summary and conclusions

How pleased will buyers be if they know you have read this book? Distraught that their secrets have been let out of the bag? Delighted that they at last have someone who recognizes their pressured agenda, and might just be able to help them with it? If it is the former, then it is as well that you *have* read it; you will need all of its advice to handle such a competitive, perhaps confrontational, beast. If it is the latter, be equally delighted, but make sure that the lessons are learned.

This concluding chapter provides a 10-point checklist to be used as a summary, as an aid to preparation, and, it is to be hoped, as a foundation for building a positive relationship with your opposite number.

The ten-point checklist

1. How does my customer organize their *purchasing processes*?
   – What are the key processes on which they focus?
   – Against which can I distinguish and differentiate my offer?
   – How do my contacts fit into the 'snail', and how could I improve my understanding of the 'real' needs of the customer and still work *through* the buyer?
2. What is the overriding (purchasing) *strategy of my customer*? Is it a cost leader, an innovation leader, an account with overall growth, global/regional or local? Is this customer diversifying or focusing more on a limited market area? What are key attributes of this account, and how does my company fit this (potential) customer profile?

3. Where is my customer's *purchasing development*?
   - Where is the customer's buying organization in terms of purchasing maturity, and more importantly, are there indications that change is on the horizon? If so, do these new steps provide me with opportunities or risks, and what and where do I need to prepare in order to be ready in time?
   - Does the customer (not a specific buyer, but the customer organization) have a price, cost or value focus? Based on their focus, how can we begin to build or defend our value?
   - What is the buying set-up of the customer (for example local, lead buying, corporate or service centre), and what does this mean for my contact matrix and selling investments? Who are the key decision makers?

4. How can I improve the *interaction with the buyer*?
   - What is the buyer's profile, and how must I respond in order to create and demonstrate value?
   - Do I understand what is important to the buyer? How does their reward scheme work? What are their hidden needs?

5. How does the buyer view my items, and how in the mind of the buyer does my company fit into the supplier portfolio? What is the *buyer's analysis of the sourcing situation*?
   - How important are my items in terms of spend compared with other items (using a Pareto/ABC analysis)?
   - *The key analysis (Kraljic):* Where does the buyer see my impact on the bottom line and the supply risk, and what sourcing strategy will they therefore follow for my different items? Could I reconstruct the analysis from the actions that I see the buyer taking? Do I oversell or undersell the value of my items? Could I benefit from linking different items that are in different areas of the sourcing matrix?
   - How does the buyer's sourcing matrix fit with my own sales importance analysis?
   - How does the buyer view my importance in the supplier portfolio? Judging by their actions, am I treated as a 'partner' (do I have the associated benefits or just the 'nice words'?), a challenger (and is there joint progress against that?) or am I a support supplier? Where do I want to be and how do I get there?
   - Does the relationship I experience match with the item characteristics and the sourcing situation? If not, how could I influence or adjust this?
   - What does the Porter five-forces analysis look like for this customer and this item? What are the customer's activities on sourcing (alternative suppliers/alternative products)?
   - How does this customer select suppliers? How do the criteria fit with my strengths and weaknesses? Key question: is there a cultural fit?

6. Although I am of course an expert in *negotiations*, where can I improve?
   - How could I better use the three-step proces, and specifically the diagnosis and conditioning phase, the implementation phase and aftercare, to ensure ongoing success?
   - How could I work the buyer's tactics to my advantage?
7. Are there any key lessons on how my company *manages buyers in terms of pricing*?
   - Is the pricing relation correct (cost-plus or value), and do all players in the game understand the impact?
   - Are the timing and communication geared to success? If not, what is the right timing? Do I understand the timing of my customers?
8. Does the *purchasing agenda* of a *specific customer* give me any opportunity to increase the selling value?
9. Do I need to review the *buying and selling relationship* with this customer? Do I need to move away from a traditional relationship towards some form of account management?
10. How can I raise the status of my buyer?
    - Is it possible to act as a bridge between the buyer and their own colleagues?
    - Will their decision in my favour serve to enhance their reputation with their colleagues, and if it does, am I promoting that fact wide and far?
    - Have I remembered that, like most mortals, buyers have personal and career ambitions that I can influence?

As a final thought, imagine you were to swap jobs with a buyer tomorrow – you are the poacher turned gamekeeper, they get the car and the expense account. Now ask yourself, and be honest: would the same outcomes result? Would the same sales be made, and at the same prices and terms? Would the same opportunities be discussed and chased? Would the same negotiations ensue? Who can say, except we think we all will mostly conclude: absolutely not! For one thing, what will happen when the seller (that's the ex-buyer of course) gets up and walks out of the negotiation?

If we believe that there will be different outcomes (perhaps better, perhaps worse, but that is not the point), then that is because we recognize the different perspectives each would bring to their new tasks. This is not to say that we have two personalities at work who could never think or work in anything but their original role – give this experiment three months and we suspect each will have conformed to the type conditioned by their new role – but that at least in the first week or so we will have two different thought processes at work, driven by two different views of the world.

This is why it is so important for sales people to have a better understanding of buyers. This is why we wrote this book. If by recognizing the agenda of buyers the seller can modify their words, their behaviours, and their actions, then they stand a much better chance of turning the 'blocker' buyer into the 'enabler' buyer, so helping to open up the customer, and all its opportunities, to your true value.

Value is irrelevant if it does not reach its intended recipient, and it can be destroyed at many points in that journey. Buyers will readily destroy it if it seems to them that it is being touted by sellers with no reference to their own needs – this is the value-meltdown scenario. By becoming 'relevant' to the buyer, the sales professional makes such a scenario less likely, and when value becomes important to the buyer the threat is banished.

We will not wish you 'good luck' with your buyers; this 10-point checklist removes the necessity for the stars to smile kindly on you. It will help you to make your own luck, provided of course that you are wide-awake to the rationale behind each question and each point. We trust our wake-up call will ensure that this is so.

14 Getting further help

As well as developing your understanding of the modern buyer, we hope that this book has sparked a desire in you to do something about that new perspective. So, what next?

Reading list

You might like to explore further, and the following books and articles will be of use. We also list here references for some of the main sources used in writing this book:

Cheverton, Peter (2007) *Global Account Management: Big customers – shrinking world*, Kogan Page, London

Cheverton, Peter (2008) *Key Account Management: The route to profitable key supplier status*, 4th edn, Kogan Page, London

Kraljic, P (1983) Purchasing must become supply management, *Harvard Business Review*, September/October

Treacy, M and Wiersema, F (1995) *The Discipline of Market Leaders*, Harper-Collins, London

van Weele, A J (1994/1999/2001/2005) *Purchasing and Supply Chain Management: Analysis, planning and practice*, 4th edn, Cengage, London

References

Dupont (early 20th century) *Return on Investment*, Du Pont Powder Company, Wilmington, Delaware, and adaptations by many others

Monczka, R M (1999) 'What is so exciting about purchasing', *Quality Matters*, Philips Electronics, January.

Pareto, V (1897) 'The new theories of economics', *Journal of Political Economy*, volume 5.

Porter, M E (1985) Competitive Advantage: Creating and sustaining superior performance, Free Press, New York.

Purspective (2000) *Dutch Windmill*, Purspective, Waardenburg, The Netherlands (adaptation of the Kraljic Matrix).

van Weele, A J (2000), *Purchasing and Supply Management; Analysis and practice*, Business Press, Eindhoven.

van Weele, A J and Rozemeijer F A (1996) *Revolution in Purchasing: Building competitive power through proactive purchasing*, Philips Electronics/Eindhoven University of Technology, Eindhoven.

Training

In our experience perhaps the most impactful and valuable training received by sales professionals is in this area: understanding buyers and knowing how to build value with them.

The best of such training events are where sellers get to role-play with real buyers, and where they also have a chance to experience the buyer's role in reverse role plays. When this is done using the company's own buyers the results can be doubly rewarding.

INSIGHT Marketing and People has developed a strong reputation in developing such training, and if this is interesting to you please feel free to contact us:

INSIGHT Marketing and People Ltd
Insight House
11 Stour Close
Slough
Berkshire
SL1 2TU
United Kingdom
Tel: +44 (0)1753 822990
Fax: +44 (0)1753 822992
e-mail: customer.service@insight-mp.com
website: www.insightmp.com

Speak to your own buyers

It's free (as far as we know), and hugely revealing to both parties!

Index